TENTH
LEGION

Books by Tom Kelly

Tenth Legion

Dealer's Choice

Better on a Rising Tide

The Season

The Boat

TENTH LEGION

TIPS, TACTICS, AND INSIGHTS ON TURKEY HUNTING

With a New Preface by Tom Kelly

Tom Kelly

THE LYONS PRESS
Guilford, Connecticut
An imprint of The Globe Pequot Press

The Lyons Press is an imprint of The Globe Pequot Press.

10 9 8 7 6 5 4 3 2

Printed in the United States of America

Design by Sans Serif, Inc., Saline, Michigan

ISBN-13: 978-1-59228-601-0
ISBN-10: 1-59228-601-1

The Library of Congress has previously cataloged an earlier
(hardcover) edition as follows:

Kelly, Tom, 1927–
    Tenth legion / Tom Kelly.
      p. cm.
    Originally published: Brooklyn : T. Gaus's Sons, 1973.
    ISBN-10: 1-55821-539-5
    1. Turkey Hunting. I. Title.

SK325.T8K455
598.6'45—dc21   97-19704
                                                  CIP

NOTE

None of the characters in this book are in any way fictional or imaginary. All of them are real people who have been known to the author for years.

Statements made herein concerning timber, people, or the physiological processes of turkeys are matters of opinion and are subject to discussion.

Statements made herein concerning the thought processes of turkeys, or of deer hunters, are known scientific facts and are not open to question.

The author declines to debate the accuracy of these with anyone.

He is, however, perfectly willing to fight about them.

CONTENTS

PREFACE TO THE 2005 EDITION

Thirty-two years ago, when I first did this book, I made no attempt to find a publisher for two reasons.

It was my opinion that there were so few turkey hunters to write for that the market did not even qualify as a niche, but might best be called a sliver. And secondly, considering the stuff that was being written thirty-two years ago about turkeys, there was no publishing concern in the country qualified to comment on the quality of the manuscript, except for its literary worth of course, and it most certainly was not being written for the literary community.

It was being written for the brethren.

It has poked along for more than thirty years now, refusing to die, and evidently, there are more of you out there than I thought there were. Finally, there may be some of the first glimmerings of hope.

I cannot prove the following statement, even though I believe it, but I am convinced that at least half the turkeys killed in the southeast today are being shot over green fields and chufa patches— which is simply baiting six months before the fact—or are called to the gun by someone other than the shooter. Both of which actions qualify as examples of opportunistic execution rather than turkey hunting and are exactly similar to the actions of the man who operates the guillotine. He simply trips the switch that removes the head. Other parties got the head in position for the removal.

The use of turkey decoys in the afternoon, recently legalized in Alabama, is a case in point. An entire state has simply given these executioners another weapon.

Turkey hunting is not fair. It would be fair if you could fly and the turkey could shoot back. But it ought to be made as sportsmanlike as possible and this continual easing of rules and cutting of corners is wholly inappropriate.

The fact that this little book has gone through nine printings is some small indication of hope. It hints that somewhere out there, there are tiny oases of culture in the howling deserts of barbarism.

If you are a member of one of these tiny groups, welcome.

If you are one the opportunistic executioners, there may still be time.

Go and repent.

PREFACE TO THE 1998 EDITION

Theo Gaus's Sons, who operated out of 30 Prince Street, in Brooklyn, advertised themselves as "Limited Edition Book Printers since 1874."

The phrase *Limited Edition Printers* is, of course, a euphemism for those concerned with printing books for which the author thinks he may not be able to find a publisher, but which contain ideas he feels are sufficiently important for him to be willing to pay the publishing costs himself.

In August of 1973, I paid Theo Gaus's Sons the total amount of $1211.25, which included freight, for 555 copies of *Tenth Legion*. The original order was for 500. There were fifty-five extras that were sent at no extra cost.

I proposed to sell the book for $4.95, which would give me my bait back upon the sale of the 245th copy.

It was my opinion at the time that there were nearly 200 guys who were not aware that I could read and write, and native curiosity would cause most of them to buy the book. I figured that even if things stopped there, I had a lifetime supply of Christmas presents already in hand and would recoup the balance of the money in the form of saving wear and tear on the nervous system during the annual Christmas shopping season.

Things worked out better than I thought they would, since the book has been in print continuously for all of the twenty-five years that have elapsed since August of 1973, and has gone through seven printings, every one very small, every one done by a ragtag collection of pseudo-publishers, one of which for a length of time that spanned a couple of editions, this one being a law firm in Louisiana.

Finally, after twenty-five years of common-law irregularity, a legitimate publishing firm has made an honest woman of it.

There is an old story to the effect that if you persist in eating soup out of doors, there will be periods when rainfall during mealtime will make it difficult to finish. The quality of the soup diminishes but the volume holds its own.

We know a good deal more about turkeys than we did twenty-five years ago, but there have not been enough changes to make the book so far out-of-date that it has become invalid. The people, of course, are just as feckless and irresponsible as ever.

The soup remaining in the bowl, though aged past the first peak of freshness and no longer of its original strength, is still perfectly acceptable.

And this time, wrapped as we are in the cloak of legitimacy, there is no need to worry about the bait.

—Tom Kelly
Spanish Fort, Alabama

PREFACE TO THE FIRST EDITION

There is a peculiarity about military organizations that defies explanation.

This peculiarity is that when a unit has once achieved real distinction, once it has become really good, rather than simply thinking it is good—it stays good.

When there is nothing left of the original organization but the signs and the flags, the previously established reputation feeds upon itself. The people who formed this reputation, the men who created the excellence, may have been dead and gone a hundred years; but if the excellence they first created was good enough, it is of itself self-perpetuating.

Perhaps the reputation inspires the men who follow. Perhaps because of it, the men who follow rise above themselves to match it. But at any rate it happens, and it has been happening for a very long time. For example:

At the Normandy landings in 1944, the right flank regiment at Omaha Beach was the 116th Infantry. It was taken temporarily from its parent division, selected solely because of its excellence, and attached to another division and put into this situation.

Its performance was superior, as it was only to be expected that it should have been. Eighty-two years previously its performance had likewise been superior. Eighty-two years previously the 116th Infantry had been the Stonewall Brigade.

When a small city-state in middle Italy conquered the world, and kept it conquered for five centuries, historians agree generally that of all the Roman Legions, there was none to match the Tenth.

Generation after generation, in country after country, and against successive waves of barbarians, there was always the Tenth.

Three hundred years after the formation of the original Tenth, when no great-grandfather left alive could remember the great-grandson of the youngest man of the original group, the legend of the Tenth grew and fed upon itself and was self-sustaining.

An organization such as this is a subculture, a cult that exists within a larger group. It can happen, though it is less common, in organizations other than military ones.

In South Alabama, in the hunting of a particular species of game bird, there is such a cult.

And it is this cult, this spiritual descendant of the original Tenth, that is the subject of our discussion.

PEOPLE

In the southern part of the United States there lives a remarkable bird. A bird that has lived wild in the woods for centuries. A bird who no less an authority than Benjamin Franklin put forth in candidacy as the national emblem of our country. A bird who, hatched in May, will at the end of the first summer weigh ten pounds. A bird with a long neck and legs, a blue head, and with breast and back feathers of a subdued though iridescent beauty. A bird who when grown to a weight of twenty pounds can fly at a speed of 50 miles an hour, through trees. A bird whose sense of hearing is simply phenomenal, whose sense of sight is even better than that, and who bears about the same resemblance to the barnyard turkey as I do to Jack Dempsey—in his prime.

The name of this bird is *Meleagris gallopavo sylvestris*, the Eastern Wild Turkey.

Concerning this bird, his habits and his traits, his life cycle and his range, and about the skill required in matters pertaining to his pursuit and capture there has arisen a mystique. A mystique that has grown into a deviant subculture.

Such is the depth of this mystique, and so thick is the veil before the truth, that before the creature can even be approached with a modicum of reason and logic, it becomes necessary to peel away the layers of legend—much as one peels the skin from around an onion.

And because the legend has been created so largely by the

men who hunt him, and the actions of these men, it therefore becomes necessary to attempt to dissect the men, before you can examine the bird.

Let me begin by admitting that any participant in blood sports is an anachronism. Any man who hunts, hunts in order to kill, no matter what he says about it. Regardless of the ceremonies that surround a sport, regardless of the complexities, and some of them are most remarkably complex, and despite the artificial rules the participants erect for one another, the ultimate aim of a blood sport is the death of a beast. A great many of the participants in blood sports, the honest ones, not only recognize this, they enthusiastically embrace it. They neither make specious rationalizations about the inherent cruelty of nature, nor about the necessity of harvesting excess stocks of birds or animals. They submit to game laws and to closed seasons and they pay their money only in order that there may continue to be huntable populations. They approach the killing with anticipation and in the event the kill is successfully made, feel absolutely no remorse—only a sensation of satisfaction and fulfillment. Men who deny this basic truth lie. Men who do not wish to kill need only to stop. The ultimate difficulty that you can build into the game is not to play it at all.

We who do play it, must play on our terms and under our own conditions and it must be within our rules. There may be so much difficulty built into it that in the end it becomes rather formal and stylized. But no matter what some of us may say, all of us hunt primarily to kill.

If this admission makes us bloody-minded and heavy-handed barbarians, so be it. It is always best to begin honestly.

In my state there are two broad groups of serious hunters, and some sidelines. Everybody shoots doves because the season opens early and it is a social function. Boys primarily hunt squirrels and rabbits. There are some fox hunters and some coon hunters. There are, or used to be, some dedicated duck hunters, and there are still some few old line quail hunters, though these last are primarily dog owners. Specialized dog owners, perhaps, but dog owners nevertheless. In quail hunting, the bird is a necessary marker in the game to ascertain the worth of the dog. Like money in poker, it measures the value of the hand.

2

The serious hunters here, though, are of two kinds. Those who hunt deer and those who hunt turkeys. By far the overwhelming number of disciples that follow either of these two religions follow that of deer hunting.

I have no real argument with these people. I am aware that deer hunting as it is done in the Northeast or in the West is both a demanding and a skillful occupation—but not here—not as it is done in Alabama. As a member of a spiritual Tenth Legion, a group who like Galahad, pursue the Grail, I look upon this other, lesser sect, with a degree of awe, but not with envy.

Let us digress from the main business at hand for a moment or two and discuss these curious specimens—anthropology is almost always absorbingly interesting—and go in imagination with them on a typical deer hunt.

They arise, like wives in the Bible, while it is yet night. They sally forth into the darkness with a remarkable amount of door slamming and racket, leaving a sleepless house behind them, wearing expensive boots and heavy clothes and burdened down with large boxes of hogmeat and whiskey. They drive for hours through the predawn darkness and finally arrive at their hunting ground, a place normally equipped with a club house. There they build immense fires, both in the fireplace inside and in the yard outside. They stand around these fires drinking coffee and discussing the relative merits or demerits of certain breeds of hounds and the supposed superiority of No. 1 to No. 00 buckshot. Those of the group who drove up the night before and spent the night in the club house hold contests inside to see who can eat the most greasy eggs. More carloads of men and additional truckloads of dogs arrive continuously, each adding to the crowd and to the tumult. Invariably several dog fights break out between the various groups of dogs brought from different ends of the county.

Ultimately the eggs are all eaten, the fires die, the dogs are thrashed into silence and the hunt committee retires into the club house. They go there into executive session, and after a great deal of consultation, conflicting opinions and pooling of ignorance, lay out the hunt. The committee comes forth finally with the hunt plan and with a hatful of numbered tickets. Upon these tickets are written the numbers of the stands. A stand is where you stay during a deer drive. It is a remarkable example of inept naming because by rights it ought to be called either a sit or a bore, since so much of both happen there so often. But it is not, and since we are in Rome. . . .

Before the hunters draw their stands from the hat there is usually a welcoming speech by the club president, or the hunt-master, and a discussion of local ground rules concerning what will or will not be shot, and why. The hunters draw the stands from the hat then, and after no little swapping of numbers and expressions of dissatisfaction they are, with enormous confusion, shouting and considerable sorting out by the numbers, loaded into the back of various pickup trucks, jeeps and other four-wheel drive vehicles. The rolling stock will be used to transport them to the numbered stands, for deer hunters, like caged hens, do not like to let their feet touch the nasty ground any more than is absolutely necessary.

They are all carried out into the woods along roads and are dropped off in order at their respective stand numbers, usually tags nailed to trees, and are sternly forbidden to move.

In most cases, at the same time this operation is going on, the drivers release the dogs through error. These are the drivers of the deer, not of the trucks. Mostly they are leathery, grizzled types, wearing overalls and carrying old, worn, professional-looking shotguns. They are local residents, neighbors of the club who are not members, but who have been especially re-cruited for the occasion and who know the hunting grounds thoroughly, a knowledge mostly acquired by years of poaching. Not only will two or three of these gentlemen kill a deer, but some of them will neglect to bring it in, and will pick it up later in the day when they return to gather up the lost dogs.

The early and erroneous release of the dogs, which happens so often as to be almost normal, or possibly even deliberate, causes dogs, deer, drivers, pickup trucks and standers all to be in motion simultaneously, although scattered over two sections, and creates vast amounts of dissatisfaction later at the post mortem, when everybody gets mad at everybody else.

Finally all the standers are placed and all the dogs are in action, except those who have very wisely lain down in the nearest sunny spot and thoughtfully gone to sleep, and the hunt is on.

The hunt moves gradually from a plateau of boredom to a

crescendo of tedium and then culminates into an interminable session of sitting on stands listening to dogs bark. Dogs run back and forth in front of and behind the standers. They run on both sides. The standers sit—they stand—they fidget and smoke. They get up to watch birds and squirrels. They wander around and around their tree and kick the leaves. During cold weather some of them build small fires. Some of them who shouldn't, but do, drink from time to time surreptitiously from flat brown bottles. Shots are heard periodically, the location of which will become the subject of exhaustive questions and discussions later on. Dogs pass, both walking and running, some silent, some vocal, and occasionally the standers see drivers moving through the woods shouting directions to each other. In certain cases dogs come up to the stand and lie down to rest gratefully.

Eventually sometime during the course of all these thrilling events, one or another of the dogs will run somebody's deer past somebody's stand where the stander has spent the morning scratching both his ass and his leaves. At a range of thirty yards, with buckshot, in a dazzling display of marksmanship, the creature is shot down. The hunter goes then and cuts the deer's throat with the long knife most deer hunters seem compelled to carry on their belt, drags the carcass back to the stand, and sits down to await the coming of the truck with precisely the same self-satisfied air as a Neanderthal who has just killed a hairy mammoth with two rotten sticks and a rock.

Much, much later in the day the vehicle returns for the stander, and to a chorus of silence from the unsuccessful standers already aboard, the deer is loaded into the back of the truck. It is carried then in triumph back to the club house and still later in the day, after all the blowflies have come from adjoining counties to get a good shot at it, is skinned and haggled into chunks by a collection of drunks with rusty saws and old dull hatchets.

Now the real business of the day begins. Barbecue is served, and it is usually delicious barbecue. The one thing this group really does well is eat. Whiskey is drunk for the first time openly, in vast quantities. The kangaroo court is formed, normally with the most obnoxious extrovert of the lot on the bench, and the suspected location of mysterious shots is dis-

5

cussed until reason totters. Persons who admit to having killed a deer for the first time have their faces bloodied and have substantial quantities of deer guts rubbed into their hair. Guts from the lower part of the intestinal tract—guts full of deer shit. Lies are told concerning the actions of adjoining standers, and crimes both actual and fancied are exhaustively researched and punished. Shirt tails are cut off, in some cases level with the shoulder blades. Interminable and boring discussions of lost dogs begin, and the early strategy for the dog hunt is planned, an activity that will keep certain of the drivers in the woods for the next two or three days, since fully half the dogs ran into the adjoining township—barking, until they passed from hearing and have not yet returned.

The crowd grows progressively drunker and it is usually at about this time that the first tempers are lost. Little groups begin to form, and the humor, and that should definitely be in quotation marks, gets progressively more and more heavy-handed.

Finally, long after the threshold of gluttony has not only been crossed, but overrun, the hunters gather up their bloody pieces of deer neckbone and brisket and start home. There is a great deal of exchanging of remnants of bottles and a resupply of paper cups so that no car leaves without a drink or two all around for the trip home, something they all need so badly.

Upon arriving at their various homes after dark, finally, smelling like bushels of rotting apples, they go in through the back door and stand in the kitchen with the gristly meat wrapped in old pieces of newspaper and dripping blood on the floor. When the wife raises one eyebrow and looks "well," they are able to expand their chests with a sackful of masculine pride and say proudly,

"We got six."

Look carefully at that pronoun if you will. And notice something else. The next time you are thrown into the company of a collection of these unfortunates, observe closely the set of the head and the expression around the eyes—especially around the eyes as they draw their stand numbers before the hunt. Now think back.

They exhibit precisely the same expressions and exactly the same behavior patterns that you saw in soldiers standing in line before G.I. whorehouses during World War Two. It forces you to the inescapable conclusion that the thought processes of the two groups are as alike as their facial expressions. Neither group has any interest in, nor time for, the thrill of the chase. They demand, and are willing to pay for, guaranteed success.

Their kind of deer hunting guarantees success. Somebody is surely going to kill one, and all the hunters can bring some fragment of the kill home. Furthermore, since the entire hunt can be included in the pronoun we, no one will ever be left out. Everybody is a winner.

After carefully considering the matter for some years, I have reached the inescapable conclusion that the principal difference between deer hunters and the soldiers in line at the whorehouse I just mentioned, lies in the different type of trophy they each bring home.

To be perfectly honest about it too, a piece of bloody neckbone, unpalatable though it may be, is after all much more desirable than a case of the clap, so that deer hunting does have a real advantage after all.

God, in His infinite wisdom, furnishes harmless and suitable amusements for all of His lesser creations.

I am, of course, overdrawing this a little, but only a very little. There are some hunting clubs that stalk hunt, and some that do not allow drinking, and there are some preachers who deer hunt and who don't drink. Believe me, I have never objected to the whiskey. If you go on one of these affairs you have to drink to be able to stand it.

The principal point to be taken is the basic psychological difference between two classes of people, those who deer hunt and those who do not. If you have read all this carefully and believed 15 percent of it, the next time someone asks you if you would like to go on a Southern deer hunt, you can say,

"No, thank you, I've already been."

Turn now over to the other side of the coin and visit for a while with a member of the Tenth Legion, one of the Lord's anointed.

He too arises while it is yet night, but he does it quietly. Not only does he get up and drive in the night but he gets into the woods while it is still night. I don't mean in the woods in his car, I mean in the woods on his feet, off the road. And believe it or not, in this day and age, he is alone—in the dark. By himself. With no roaring fire and no cups of coffee and no collection of companions to keep up a running fire of inanities to keep him from thinking. He understands quite clearly that if he does happen to kill a turkey he is going to have to work for it, and even beyond that he knows he is going to have to walk to it. He also knows that when he comes back home empty-handed, as he will do regularly, he will have no satisfactory explanation. He is well aware, for he has met dozens of them, of the numbers of people that will approach him on street corners and in bars and at parties, who will open each conversation with,

"Well, did you get him yet?"

When he answers no, they will be off and running. They will tell him in delighted tones and in the clearest detail the story of a friend of theirs who has a feeble-minded nephew. Of how this nephew is occasionally allowed home on leave from the state funny farm. How that the last time this poor defective creature was home, week before last, he went out in the woods just behind the house, sat on a log, and with a turkey yelper that was given away as a souvenir by a typewriter company in 1937, yelped twice, and killed a turkey that weighed twenty-three pounds—picked.

Various and sundry of these individuals will approach him full of stories, which they will insist upon telling, of nine-year-old girls who killed nineteen pound gobblers; of little old ladies from Arkansas (they do leave off the tennis shoes) who killed two with one shot; and of log truck drivers in the northern part of the county who ran over a roadful of turkeys last week and killed three.

Never in all of recorded history has one of these street corner turkeys weighed less than eighteen pounds.

Every bit of this must be accepted in silence since there is no adequate answer, but the expression on the face of the listener will be very like that of a water bird who is being offered a spoiled frog.

When our hero finally does achieve social acceptability by killing a turkey, he will be searched out and told in delighted tones by one of these talkative creatures how only that morning Sam Johnson killed his third of the season—all three of which were monsters.

None of these lovely people hunt turkeys. I have never been exactly sure where they live, for they are never in evidence in the summertime, but usually appear only in the spring and fall. Like the lilies of the field, they toil not, neither do they spin, but appear to exist only to discuss turkeys. And they are not arrayed in any glory either.

A member of the legion has to learn to endure these slings and arrows with outward aplomb. He has to do so because he soon learns that during the turkey season the communication channels will be largely blocked except those that exist with sinners like himself.

He knows that his wife, his family, his associates and his employer, if he is fortunate enough to reach the end of the season still employed, will view the close of the season with paeans of joy and thanksgiving equal to those with which he and the rest of the legion viewed its approach.

He will experience moments of tragedy of such a depth and feeling as to preclude them from having been written by anyone but Euripides, and he will exalt in periods of piercing rapture previously understood only by willing Christian martyrs being eaten by willing lions. He will operate primarily in a climate not of desire but of compulsion. This is painfully evident in my own case. I do not hunt turkeys because I want to, I hunt them because I have to. I would really rather not do it, but I am helpless in the grip of my compulsion. In some fortunate people the compulsion is a trifle more well adjusted than in others, but only a trifle.

In our previous discussion of deer hunters I did overdraw things just a little. In this case, I have understated it by as much.

Crops have been lost hunting turkeys and wives estranged. Fairly close relatives have gone into the grave at unattended funerals, except on extremely rainy days and businesses have gone to rack and ruin unless sustained by sympathetic companions or by associates who understand compulsions they do not share.

I speak none of this in apologia, mind you. We need no apology. Subcultures exist in all societies.

Not that it is the only yardstick of comparison but turkey hunting as a cult does have substantial advantages over chasing girls. To adjust a quotation from Lord Chesterfield, not only is the position not nearly so ridiculous but the expense is not so damnable. The pleasure is much less fleeting, and high on the list of its principal advantages is that a gentleman may discuss his conquests afterward.

Turkey hunters love to talk about it. In fact they talk about it all the time. Especially in the spring, when the volume of telephonic gossip concerning who heard what where, and who saw who when, has had as much to do with making AT&T a blue chip in this state as has that company's business acumen.

In all these discussions hunters are usually just as quick to admit defeat as they are to relate triumph. And, except for those strange individuals who murder turkeys out of car windows or from boat seats or who lie around the edges of pastures with rifles, there is always a curious humility in these confessions. The bird possesses a remarkable ability to turn arrogance into hopelessness. Other members of the lodge are perfectly willing to listen to these tales of frustration and tragedy because they understand quite well that the day will surely come when the table turns, and they are going to get to tell them while someone else listens.

You should accept all these statements, or whatever part of them you find you can comfortably swallow, with liberal helpings of salt. Normally the most congenial of men, easygoing and biddable to the point of wishy-washiness, I am the first to admit what must have become evident with crystal clarity several paragraphs ago. I find it necessary to approach certain important matters with the same stiff-necked, opinionated positiveness as did those Roman Senators who prefaced every public utterance for two centuries with the preamble, "Carthage must be destroyed!"

And the subject of turkeys, because of its supreme importance, I do so approach.

2

TURKEYS AND PEOPLE

I first came to an awareness of turkeys sometime during the late 1930's. I became aware at that time that there were people who hunted them seriously, people who went out and deliberately did it. I had an uncle who was so afflicted.

Insofar as present day turkey hunters are concerned, the decade of the 1930's constitutes the darkest of the dark ages. The legendary numbers that William Bartram heard in 1776, when he wrote how at daylight during March and April the woods remained in a continuous shout for over an hour, were all gone. The vast droves that our grandfathers had shot into were gone too. They had largely disappeared with the disappearance of the virgin timber some few years after World War One. There were a great many things that caused this. There is strong evidence to suggest that there was an introduction of fowl pox from domestic stock. It is evident that there was a marked change in timber type and forest cover, a change from old growth to second growth, a situation which the bird had later to adapt to, a situation we will look into in a minute. And certainly there existed in 1930 a rural population that in many cases was composed of individuals who killed thirty or forty birds a year.

All of the reasons for the decline are not known. All of them will probably never become known, but the numbers of turkeys declined sharply, and due to whatever known and unknown combination of causes, the period between 1925 and 1945 saw turkey populations reach the lowest ebb of all.

In a great many areas the bird absolutely vanished.

Sections of the state that formerly had hillsides that looked as if they had been raked and piled from turkey scratching in the fall, and that had resounded to multiple gobbles in the spring, lay undisturbed and silent.

Looking back at the period now, from a distance of thirty years, it is evident that the bird as a species was pushed very nearly to the edge of extinction.

There are, you see, two kinds of extinction, practical and biological. Whooping cranes, for instance, have been in a condition of practical extinction for some several years. The few scattered flocks that remain are simply creatures in a zoo, a zoo without bars. Before any species of bird or animal vanishes, there is a point beyond which, if the numbers fall, recovery cannot be accomplished, and practical extinction then becomes biological. How close turkeys must have come to biological extinction is problematical. In many states they did achieve this dubious distinction and vanished, and only until recent reintroductions have they returned.

At any rate, in this state, scattered colonies of turkeys existed in some of the backwoods, heavily timbered counties and along some of the major river bottoms, and oddly enough the season was never closed. It unquestionably should have been, but it never was, and I think the danger point came and passed and no one was ever aware just how close we really came.

In short, a late-thirties turkey hunter was a man apart. Except for those very few fortunate individuals who hunted on closely guarded and controlled land, a man who heard a turkey gobble had had a successful hunt. A man who killed one every two or three years was an outstanding success. A man who killed one annually was almost a national monument and could have had a fence built around him and made a living charging admissions to tourists for interviews. The average hunter was a man who, like one of the pair of mythical Japanese lovers condemned to ten thousand years in separate hells, lived in the hope of better things to come but had little expectation of any immediate change.

Turkey hunters of the 1930's lived on speculation and they

lived on memory. They hunted in places where they were morally certain there were no longer turkeys, but like playing in the crooked game, they did it because it was the only game in town. Some of them grew old and quit. Some of them died and quit. Some of them despaired and quit. A few, a very pitiful and dedicated few, carried on.

Sometime right after the Second World War, and for reasons nobody clearly understood, a few people began to kill turkeys. Nobody was doing anything different, it just began to happen. An occasional turkey would be killed on a deer drive—it was legal then. A squirrel hunter would shoot one off the limb at daylight or kill one flying up to roost at dark. Boys who were poking along creeks in the upper coastal plain, jump-shooting wood ducks, began to flush an occasional turkey off a sand bar on the creek and kill him. Turkeys were seen in the morning by logging crews on their way to work, and turkey tracks began to appear in woods roads where none had been seen for twenty years. The open season, which had existed on the books largely as two academic dates with a practical void between them, took on meaning, added flesh and red blood to the skeleton, and rose vigorously from the sepulchre.

By this time, by and large, the old breed of hunters were no longer active, "age had made their custom stale and withered their variety," but there did remain in scattered areas and sections some of them yet. Some of them remained as yeast cells, available to pass on information to the new breed, much as the making of pottery was passed on by word of mouth in certain Indian tribes for centuries.

Some of these people brought their creaky old bones out of retirement and took sons, or nephews, or the sons of old friends into their confidence and shared nearly lost skills. And to these few we owe a remarkable debt of gratitude.

Some of them came out of retirement and possibly because of regret and bitterness over their lost youth became secretive. They gave advice like, "You ain't covering enough ground and you ain't yelping enough."

Some of them, who never had known anything about hunting turkeys in the first place, surfaced, delighting in their newly found and richly undeserved status as senior experts and

13

founts of wisdom, and passed on legend, misinformation and ignorance.

The world being the kind of place that it is, this last class was by far the most numerous. Some of the ignorance and misinformation thus transmitted to us innocents was astounding. You would not believe the number of stories I have heard that began with, "There I was, sitting in a clump of gallberry bushes," in areas a hundred miles north of the last known occurrence of gallberry. The number of these gentlemen who acted as if they were carryovers from the days of Boone and Crockett, rather than from 1925, was simply unbelievable. Many, many of them, separated from their peers by a quarter of a century, and with nobody left alive to tell the difference, or nobody who was qualified to disagree with them, instructed and pontificated and remembered big. I can remember developing a sense of absolute pitch for these liars.

But in their defense let us consider one fact.

There are probably left alive today buffalo hunters. I am sure that if these gentlemen were asked, and being hunters, probably if they were not forcibly restrained, they would deliver lengthy dissertations on the art and skill of buffalo hunting. I really do not blame them. When I grow old I fully intend to do the same thing on other subjects. Old buffalo hunters, however, have a principal advantage in that there are no longer any buffalo left to hunt, and there are no active and participating buffalo hunters remaining in the business who have an opportunity to check the facts.

The legendary graybeards I speak of suffered from one single terrible disadvantage. They lived from one era across a hiatus into another, cast their pearls of wisdom before swine, and then found to their horror that the swine often listened and then went out and found that they had been incorrectly instructed to begin with.

There is no intention on my part to appear to be unduly harsh in discussing these old people. In most instances they served a real purpose and they did no more than many of the rest of us are someday going to do. The temptation to embroider upon and to expand the level of former and mainly imaginary glories is common to us all, especially in the absence of a check or of a contemporary who can serve as a balance.

If you will remember how it was when you were younger, the timber was bigger, the girls were prettier and more willing, you shot better, worked harder and exhibited far more gallantry in your war than do any of the unlicked cubs of today.

I, personally, am continually struck today by the remarkable degree of callow stupidity in lieutenants. Lieutenants in my day were, to a man, bright, dashing young types, packed with manly vigor and sparkling intelligence. Dedicated, superbly competent and brutally denied their rightful position of importance only because of the doddering incompetence and spiteful jealousy of worn out old crocks in their forties, a situation no longer true of course. I suspect that the miserable specimens of lieutenants extant today are caused by a little known scientific fact—the fact that gravity today is much stronger than it used to be. I am sure you must have noticed it. It undoubtedly has somehow affected both the physical and the intellectual development of our young men. It has caused me God knows how much trouble of my own lately, and I am sure that it must be affecting everyone.

In any event, the new generation of turkey hunters somehow were able to separate the diamonds from the dung. Partly due to the instruction of the saintly relics who were passing out information, and partly in spite of it, the new breed recreated a set of skills that had largely vanished with their grandfathers.

This, of course, has been a progressive process. It did not leap into being simultaneously across the country, but rather as the population level of the bird has increased area by area and county by county, the process of relearning has grown slowly behind it. I suspect that in the case of some of our less fortunate neighbors to the north, or those in adjoining states to the west, where turkey populations have only lately gotten to the point that ten-day seasons are allowable, this process of relearning is in about the same condition there as it was here in the 1950's.

We ought not to leave this subject without discussing one of the most curious anomalies of all, and that is the unwillingness of so many men to take up turkey hunting simply because of a reluctance to ask.

We are you know, after all, Americans—only two generations removed from the frontier and in certain Western states only a generation and a half. Every man Jack of us is a dead shot, an expert hunter, and everyone who was born in a town smaller than Chicago a competent and polished woodsman.

Our folklore is filled with stories similar to the one that insists that 70 percent of the German soldiers killed by the A.E.F. during World War One were shot between the eyes—with rifles. Dispassionate studies to the effect that in both that war and the two succeeding ones, three quarters of the casualties came from artillery, are simply overlooked. Such studies based on fact make only poor stories and corrupt the legend.

We believe that we are instinctively born knowing the wilderness, that we are nowhere so comfortable as in the forest primeval, and that we are quite fully capable of hunting and killing with dispatch anything from hummingbirds to elephants, even if we choose not to do it. To admit ignorance, to admit even by inference, that there is a species of game bird or animal that flies, walks, or crawls across the face of the North American continent that we are unable to hunt skillfully and kill effortlessly, somehow runs against our grain. Not only does it offend us to think it, we flatly refuse to admit that it could ever happen.

To a degree that is far more than common in this enlightened age, and only because of where I work and the people I meet in my work, I have had probably more contact with people who cannot read and write than most men of my generation have had.

I never met a man who couldn't read who came right out and said it just like that. When it finally reaches the point where it becomes necessary to discuss it, they either have to sign the timber deed or endorse the check, they invariably say, "I don't write."

Not "can't" mind you, but "don't."

And they invariably say it with the same inflection that a man uses to deny beating wives or stealing sheep or shooting orphans.

This, of course, is rationalization. It is justifiable in the case of most of my clients because it is mostly the luck of the draw. Many of these people came out of school at the age of nine to support a family. They were at nine, the oldest man the family had, and the most responsible.

16

What is strange to me though is that many men who say, "I don't hunt turkeys," say it with the same inflection.

The number of people who want to hunt turkeys and don't, because they don't know how and because they are too proud to ask, is shocking. Anybody who really wanted to could learn to do it. I will even go so far as to say that even some of those lower classes who hang about on deer stands really do have buried feelings of decency. If properly guided and encouraged, they could reform and become converted and lead valuable and constructive lives up here in the sunlight. In fact, I know they could—I have made soldiers out of worse. But for some strange reason, the simple statement that a man does not know how to hunt turkeys seems a more difficult situation for the American male to face than a state of impotence.

Some of these non-hunters are far more crafty. I have heard dozens of them say, with every evidence of sincerity, "I don't hunt turkeys in the fall because it is too easy. All you have to do is to scatter them and then call them back and kill as many as you want."

This preposterous fiction is firmly entrenched all over our area, and not only is it entrenched it is believed. Entire counties in the state forbid fall turkey hunting altogether. In recent years several counties that formerly had fall seasons have done away with them, and sportsmen's clubs are still constantly passing self-righteous resolutions against fall turkey hunting. There is precedent for this kind of thinking. I don't believe Carrie Nation ever had a drink.

I would be perfectly enchanted to go and scatter a small drove of old gobblers any December afternoon they cared to choose. The kind of turkeys that will get back together Thursday after next if they happen to think of it then. The kind of turkeys that won't yelp, and that will walk up to your yelping at the rate of 200 yards an hour. After I have scattered them I would like to invite some of these sanctimonious purists to have a shot at killing all they want.

Unless they don't want any at all, I think I could furnish them a sackful of humility and embarrassment.

All kinds of people hunt turkeys, and do it well too—log scalers, druggists, sock salesmen, bookkeepers and even vice presidents. Though honesty compels me to admit that some of the latter use callers. A caller is a man who does the work while you conduct the execution. You can do it this way—it enables you to substitute financial position for skill.

You can buy your way in, and it is not awfully expensive. Somebody to do the calling, somebody to do the scattering, or even somebody to spread the bait. Planting chufas and sitting around over them simply constitutes scattering bait for months before the fact.

You can also approach it with an initial admission of ignorance, a "put me in coach, I don't smoke," attitude, and enjoy it far more. It just depends upon what you want and how hard you are willing to work to get it.

The Sultan's son, with visiting rights in the harem for the first time, has something on his mind. A nineteen-year-old private with the afternoon off and twelve dollars in his pocket has something there too. They are both looking for the same thing. Assuming that both are successful it is not really difficult to make up your own mind as to which of them has had to exercise the superior degree of skill and gamesmanship.

Understand now, I am not in the business of going all over the country inviting people into the firm. Sometimes when I meet another man on my way to the woods, I wish everybody would quit but me.

But it is always amazing to me that this vast body of enjoyment exists, and that dozens and dozens of men will not take advantage of it simply because of a peculiar species of stiff-necked pride—largely misplaced.

3

Mostly Turkeys

Having now wandered at some length through a leisurely and somewhat waspish discussion of the people involved, let us go back to the theme of the work, the bird himself. The body of ignorance concerning the life cycle, the habits, the food preferences and the breeding practices of turkeys is vast. The state of Pennsylvania, which had its game farm program, some early work by Wheeler, a few articles by Stoddard during the mid-forties and a sprinkling of occasional papers constituted the body of knowledge until the last few years. Recently some fine substantial work is being done and very slowly now a legitimate foundation is being laid, and solid fact is replacing legend, folklore and misinformation.

The state of Florida, which always seems to have the most money, maybe because you can buy a drink there on Sunday if you want to, or get a bet down on a horse if you choose, has done more honest turkey research than anybody, anywhere. Game bird research, like all other game research, is largely paid for by hunting license fees, and because other game birds and animals are far easier to kill and are therefore more popular, they get the lion's share of the money. Florida's research, because it is their native bird, has been conducted with the subspecies Osceola, a type which does not occur here, but it is a turkey and it is legitimate turkey research, and I wish we were rich too.

Pennsylvania fostered a game farm program for some

twenty years and raised and released tens of thousands of half wild birds to feed the wildcats all over that state. As recently as a year or so ago, well meaning and misguided hunting clubs in Alabama were still doing the same thing. Hundreds of these pseudo-wild turkeys were released to introduce blackhead and fowl pox into the native flocks before they vanished into the insides of foxes and wildcats, leaving ruin and desolation in the native stock behind them. Recently, thank God, the state has taken a hand and has outlawed this nonsense. The invention of the cannon trap, a device which allows Fish and Game Departments to trap wild turkeys on a wholesale basis and to move them to other parts of the state or to adjoining states, has done more to expand the range of turkeys everywhere than any other single factor. Many people who are just now beginning to enjoy open seasons owe their seasons to the development of this device whether they realize it or not.

In my state, huntable populations of turkey existed throughout the dark period of the 1930's we have discussed. The principal reason for the bird's expansion and increase here has not been introduction but has been protection. This protection was neither enforced nor was it voluntary. It was happenstance, and it happened for an unusual reason.

During the period from 1950 to 1970, Alabama suffered a population loss of 300,000 rural citizens. This is not a percentage loss, it is a numerical loss. The state has gained very slightly in population, but only in the cities. We now have rural counties with lower populations than they had in 1920. I hold no brief that this is a desirable situation, but I have been friendly with far too many backwoods farmers and loggers not to recognize what an outstanding effect it has had on turkeys, and a beneficial effect too.

A great many of these people killed entire strings of frying-sized turkeys in August and September—strings like fish. A great many more of them killed upward of forty turkeys a year over corn-baited trenches. This was a very simple but effective operation.

You dug a shallow ditch six or eight inches wide and ten feet long and built a blind forty yards from one end and in line with the direction of the trench. You kept the ditch filled with shelled corn and when the birds began to use it regularly you waited for them one afternoon in the blind. When the trench was full of feeding heads you raked the length of it with both barrels. Then you filled up the sacks you had brought with you and went home. Not only was it quick but it saved shells.

A great many of these people were and are amazingly skillful hunters. They were patient, careful, first class woodsmen with almost unlimited time who could begin hunting at their back door. They baited and killed turkeys for meat, but they hunted them for fun, and a hell of a lot of these boys regularly called up and killed another couple of dozen gobblers every spring, besides the ones they baited.

No law enforcement program in the world could stop this then, and it could not stop it now.

I have known hundreds of these people and I know a lot of them yet, even though their numbers are diminished. They are almost without exception, honest, hardworking and fiercely proud. A man who holds their friendship may make any demand, reasonable or unreasonable, upon their time or upon their person and they will cheerfully oblige him. But they feel that fish and game and timber belong to whoever gets there first, if it is for personal use, and they think no more of game laws and bag limits than they worry over such a simple matter as the transmutation of corn into a liquid and far more valuable agricultural commodity. Nor do they give much thought as to what the balance of society thinks of either action. I am being honest when I say that some of my closest personal friends are in this group and that I not only like them, I sincerely admire them. They make the finest soldiers in the world, and they have been proving it repeatedly since the Battle of Cowpens. But in certain areas of conduct, they are simply on a different wavelength than most of the rest of us, and there is no communication possible across the chasm.

The decrease in number of this class of our population, whatever else may have resulted, has had more to do with the increase of turkeys in our state than all the cannon traps, law enforcement, good wishes of hunting clubs and firm pronouncements of sports writers put together. If you were a mathematician you could reduce it to a formula of inverse proportions.

Twenty years ago it was considered extremely fashionable

to brag about the purity of whatever strain of turkeys you happened to have to hunt, in a well-bred fashion of course. Persistent legends remain to this day to the effect that the bird we have now is not the old, true, original wild turkey. I have read some extremely learned articles, principally authored by distinguished gentlemen on the South Atlantic Coast, who insist that only in the Georgia and Carolina low country did the old, wild, pure strain of turkeys exist, uncontaminated by the infusion of domestic blood. I consider this to be the oldest, wildest, purest strain of bull shit, and I will tell you why.

First of all, I have seen, in the last ten years, the turkeys on Jekyll Island, now that the state of Georgia has bought this offshore island and turned it into a public playground. If ever there has been an example of an estate held and protected by entrenched wealth and position, committed to the denial of the presence of the unwashed, with no expense spared, this island surely qualifies. Furthermore, it is, and has been, isolated from the adulterating effects of the mainland by some fifteen miles of salt marsh, and God knows how much flowing water in sloughs and runs and salt water creeks. The turkeys I saw on this island looked exactly the same and acted exactly the same as did the ones I hunted last spring in Alabama, although the Jekyll Island turkeys had gotten used to cars and to people and seemed undisturbed by either.

Second, one of our most repetitive and persistent legends in the Southeast concerns the "mossyhead." Reputedly considerably smaller than the existing wild turkey and with feathers almost black, he is supposed to have had a black fuzz on his head, giving him the name, and a set of behavior patterns completely different from those of the existing bird. Invariably, in those late evening discussions that spring up over bourbon, some graybeard stirs the ashes and resurrects this Phoenix in solemn "it ain't like it used to be" tones.

I know men who insist they have personally killed mossyheads. I have talked to dozens more who absolutely know that it was the only true wild turkey because their grandfather told them so.

In my part of the country this, of course, settles it. The only possible remark that can be made after one of these grandfather statements is either one of submissive agreement, or the bald statement that "the old bastard was probably drunk," and this last is not considered socially acceptable.

Reflect though, for a minute upon this. William Bartram's description of the Eastern wild turkey, written in 1775, describes in precise zoological detail the bird alive today. Alexander Wilson, considered the father of American ornithology, gives a description of turkeys in the early 1800's that matches Bartram's and that clearly describes the birds killed in Alabama last spring. Audubon's famous painting of the wild turkey, done about 1820, could have been painted from a bird I saw yesterday, although Audubon's turkey was dead when painted.

Before you get mad now, the likes of me is not going to sit here in judgment on a man like John James Audubon. Any man who described in very careful detail how he shot a bushel basket of Carolina parakeets in order to see all possible varieties of plumage coloration before he drew one, does not need anybody like me to scotch for him. I will stipulate that a man who is that meticulously careful of ornithological detail is not going to miss much. But Audubon missed the shape of a turkey. He painted what he saw—and what he saw was a dead turkey on the floor in front of his easel.

When a turkey is alive the neck is long, sinuously in motion, and fluid to a degree that is nearly snakelike. When he is dead, the neck draws down into the shoulders and gives the bird a curiously humpbacked look. The turkey in Audubon's painting has exactly that humpbacked look. But leaving off the artistic criticisms of an ex-timber marker, the bird Audubon painted could have been shot this morning. In fact, it is a fine bird and I wish that I had shot it.

None of these early works discuss a mossyhead nor do they exhibit a sketch of one. And while it is theoretically possible that a sub-species existed that was missed and has become extinct, I cannot believe it.

Those early observers didn't miss any of the two pages full of the confusing fall warblers in your bird book. Bartram had an eye that described exactly the separate species of Atlantic white cedar we have in Alabama, three years after he had seen the legitimate white cedar in the Jersey swamps. So I am not willing to believe all of them missed anything as big as a subspecies of wild turkey, the maundering recollections of anybody's sainted grandfather to the contrary.

Wild gobblers do sometimes come into barnyards and mate with domestic stock. Tame men have been known to go to strange places and do as much. Upon occasion turkeys are killed that exhibit some domestic coloration. But the failure of the pen-raised birds program in so many states argues rather strongly against the part domestic thesis.

And lastly, I have seen turkey eggs found in the woods from time to time by timber markers and brought in and hatched under unwitting chickens. Anybody who has watched the conduct of one of these hatches in chicken yards, as soon as they were a week old, would have the same confidence as I do that these birds are even wilder than preachers' daughters and have not changed since the day the Vikings landed.

One of the principal factors that has led to the relatively high turkey populations in recent years and one that I have never heard discussed in ornithological circles, is the adaptability of the bird himself. The other day I read the definition of the word anthropomorphize. It means to assign to a bird or to an animal thought processes and traits that properly belong only to humans.

Biologically it is considered a sticky wicket, and professional naturalists flee it as from the wrath to come. Naturalists will carefully and precisely discuss animal behavior, the life cycle of a bird or the reproductive processes of certain species of frogs, for example, and stop. The subject has now been researched, it is now part of the world's knowledge and if the observation and the research was done logically and carefully, and it almost always is, then the matter is settled. Filed away and dropped. A law of the Medes and the Persians and not subject to change. Speaking from a firm background as an unlettered and uneducated naturalist I cannot agree.

Physiological traits yes. Behavior patterns no.

Early research, and it was very carefully done, laid great stress on the fact that it was necessary to have unbroken tracts of timbered land in blocks of 50,000 acres and upwards before turkey populations could be maintained. I live in a region that has many of its counties 80 percent timbered by land area. Turkeys live here. But turkeys in the north part of Wilcox

County, Alabama, live in farm woodlots. And in Dallas County, they live in patches and scrolls of timber interspersed among pastures in land that is 70 percent open. They can live in vast unbroken tracts of timber. But they have been demonstrating for a decade or two now that they can live in other places as well. The plain fact remains that the bird has adapted himself to an increased human population and to a variety of land uses far better than any of the early researchers were willing to give him credit for being able to do. Quite simply, he has learned.

The passenger pigeon could not adapt, and so he perished. The red cockaded woodpecker, who demands pine timber old enough to have red heart rot so he can nest in it, will become extinct if he cannot change, because today's tax structure will not let many men grow 300-year-old longleaf pine for woodpecker nests. The Everglades kite, who eats one and only one variety of freshwater snail, is standing on the ragged edge. Any life form that remains utterly dependent upon one particular situation, or upon one specific item of diet must, as a consequence, live in a state of precarious balance.

Turkeys are not like that. I am convinced that turkeys are able to learn, and that having learned, can and do change. I think that with the elimination of the virgin timber, populations continued to exist along the major river bottoms. I am convinced that in the succeeding twenty-five years or so they flourished and expanded because they learned to make do with whatever they had to live in.

The turkeys I mentioned on Jekyll Island live on lawns in a suburban housing development. While this may be an extreme case of adaptability, there are far too many turkeys alive today who never even saw 50,000 acres of old growth timber for me to accept much of that argument. I will go even farther about a turkey's ability to learn. Take, if you will, a hypothetical example.

Go to Georgia and find a flaw in the deed and take Jekyll Island away from the state. Take possession of your property and arrive one morning with two or three of your friends (you would not need your yelper to begin with) and wander through the abandoned housing development you have just acquired. Bust four or five turkeys off somebody's ex–front lawn with your twelve gauge. If you like to do it this way you had

25

better enjoy it while you can. Because in a week you would be hiding in old garages to ambush one through the window. In three months you would be right in line with the rest of us, killing one or two every spring, getting humiliated and out-thought and walked around.

I can't prove this of course. The state of Georgia is apt to turn out to be a bit sticky about giving up the island just to let me prove my point. But the bird can and will adapt just that quickly.

You ought to listen to some of this with a word of warning. Some years ago, I worked closely for a time with a governmental fish and game organization. I remember the professionals pointing out to me how they had found out years before that any man who had ever killed two squirrels considered himself an expert in game management. I know from personal experience that any man who has ever been a tenderfoot scout considers himself to be an expert in timber management, and I can show you the scars. Not only are they experts, but they know United States congressmen, and can sometimes get legislation to support the opinions they draw from their vast technical background.

Since I approach my subject with somewhat more background than most of these people, I feel qualified to be nearly as firm.

If, however, you find the hypothetical example of adaptability I just used unpalatable, try a real example of instant adaptability on for size.

Some ladies, otherwise splendid wives of turkey hunters, exhibit a peculiar reluctance to get up at three-thirty in the morning twenty or thirty times in a row and cook breakfast. Ladies, you will remember, are often subject to strange foibles. In order to help a man through this minor domestic crisis, many small towns near my home have one restaurant that opens at 3:00 A.M. on spring mornings for the sole purpose of serving breakfast to turkey hunters. On opening day it will be packed and for some two or three days thereafter will be crowded. The clientele will then diminish to some two dozen or so of the regulars. These will appear every morning, exchange stories, cry in one another's coffee, and lie and brag while they eat breakfast. They will exchange turkeys, exchange places to

hunt and take one another with one another through the balance of the season.

Some years ago, in just such a restaurant, a friend of mine
and I swapped the same turkey back and forth all spring. I
found him to begin with, the second day of the season. The first
morning he gobbled two or three times on the roost and then
pitched down to me, in range, but hidden by a little fold in the
ground. He stood around in there and strutted and drummed
for half an hour and then walked off. I had seen him in the air,
but I did not see him on the ground until he crossed the farther
ridge, out of range.

I showed up faithfully for the next three or four days,
morning and night, worked him a couple of times without success and then gave up and gave him away. The man I gave him
to worked with him a few days and then gave him back. We
played Alphonse and Gaston with that turkey throughout the
entire season and neither of us came any closer to killing him
than I did that first morning.

Both of us saw him once or twice more. He would not always gobble, but he would usually come, and then he would
walk around near enough for you to hear him drum, something
I have never been able to hear at more than eighty yards or so.
Once I had him in the open in a full strut, at ninety yards. We
both hunted other turkeys from time to time in other places, of
course, but we kept coming back to him alternately. Finally,
near the end of the season, I sank to the level of trying to meet
him at the roost when he came home from work in the evening.
I got there early one afternoon, slipped in quietly, cut and stuck
enough bushes to hide an elephant, and sat down to wait.
Every fifteen or twenty minutes I would yelp a couple of times.

He came—and during the course of the afternoon he gobbled twice, once when a crow cawed, and once very late, at an
early owl. Both times he gobbled he sounded as if he were trying to swallow the back half of it while he was regretting the
first half getting out at all. Other than that, and the fact I
thought I had heard him drum once, I neither heard him nor
saw him, but I remained convinced that he was there. At flying
up time, with a racket that was thunderous after so much stillness for so long, he flew up to roost in a clump of a half dozen
big loblolly pines that towered above some middle-sized oaks

near the bottom of a hollow. Those trees were eighteen to twenty inches in diameter and more than ninety feet tall. It was a late spring, and the woods had not yet gotten excessively thick, and the ground in there was fairly open.

I know he flew up into one of those loblollies because I saw him do it. I even heard him flopping around up there and changing limbs to get himself comfortable, even though I couldn't tell exactly which tree he was in.

And then I did a sneaky thing.

I got up, it was only just over a hundred yards away, and began to walk slowly toward the clump of pines with my gun at high port. Ethics be damned, I was going to flush him out of that tree and shoot him as he flew off. When I got within half gunshot of what I thought was his tree I slipped the safety off. When I got directly under where he had to be, I began to feel a little sorry for him, but not sorry enough to stop. I came to a stop exactly in the middle of the clump of pines and invited him in a loud clear voice to see, now, if he could make it in any direction. Stillness.

Holding the gun by its grip, in one hand, I shook bushes, kicked leaves, rattled vines and even got a stick and hammered on one of the trees with it. Nothing.

Finally I shouted.

"Shoo, you son of a bitch," in a ringing, parade ground bellow.

The stillness, if anything, deepened.

This, mind you, was a wild turkey, an old one, a turkey that you normally would expect to run a mile if you cleared your throat when you were in the same forty acres with him. I don't know yet why he wouldn't, I only know that he didn't.

As far as I know the bastard is still sitting up in that tree where I walked off and left him. He ought to be pretty hungry by now because this was ten years ago.

You may call this whatever you like. I choose to call it an instant assessment of a tactical situation and a lightning decision to take what proved to be a proper course of action.

I think that I must have gotten within forty yards of that tree before he realized what I was doing—it was beginning to get dark. I think that then he decided the best thing for him to do was to sit still, since I didn't know exactly where he was. I

28

think that he sat up there the whole time I was making a damned fool out of myself, looking down at me, and if they can laugh, laughing his wrinkled old ass off.

I hope they can laugh. I have surely furnished them a hell of a lot of funny situations during the past twenty-five years to laugh about, and I would hate to think that much opportunity for amusement has been wasted.

4

ALL TURKEYS

For a good many years I held, believed and expounded the theory that turkeys could burrow underground, like moles. I said this then, and believed it when I said it, because they had done things to me that I felt no creature could ever do on top of the ground. He would necessarily have had to use the part under the surface to do it in. In recent years it has come home to me very strongly that I was wrong. They can do it on top of the ground, and worse than that, it is not even necessary for them to extend themselves particularly to do it. They can do it as a sideline, they can do it on their way to attend to more important business. It is particularly humiliating to know that they have this capability and that besides doing what they have already done, there are God knows how many other things they are going to do to me yet, without even bothering to concentrate on it. What dreadful outrages lurk in their repertoire, if they ever bothered to give their whole concentration to fooling me, boggles the imagination.

There are though, strangely enough, stupid turkeys, or at least there are turkeys who perform irrational acts. It is a comforting chink in their armor. Some of them, like a great many men you may have met, have a tendency to open their mouths too much. And, as with younger men, the younger turkeys sin principally in this respect. Quite often in the fall, especially if he has been flushed the night before and has had ten hours in which to consider the depth of his loneliness, a young gobbler, when called to in the morning, will be pathetically willing to respond. He will come to you at your first yelp, at a run, yelping every breath, and you will have to hurry to get the gun up to shoot him before he tramples you.

Every once in a while, even in the spring when they are supposed to have more sense, you will find one gobbling on the roost in the black dark. He will act as if he not only had not had a girl all that year but the year before as well. He will double gobble at your first yelp, fly down on a long slant to save time at your second and then he will run all over you. He wants it so badly that I think he is blind, and I suspect you could stand up and wave a bed sheet, and he would still keep coming. There are not too many of them like this, but every once in a while you will find one.

Normally you are going to run across turkeys who act like this at only one time. At a time when you are already killing a lot of turkeys. During those years when you have had a spring season in which you could kill one in the backyard, or you could run over one with the car on the way to the woods. When you are going through one of those streaks when if you shoot at a flying turkey sixty yards away he instantly falls dead and when falling crashes down through dead oaks and knocks part of his feathers loose to make him easier to pick.

You have these kinds of streaks. You have others, far more common, when turkeys are impossible. If you walk into the woods in the morning, you run them off. When you try to go to them, you get too close. When you slam the car door, turkeys fly. All of the luck you had in the easy times deserts you, and the averages even out, and even and even and even. By and large, if you persevere, you are going to kill an awful lot of turkeys you didn't earn. But on the other side as well, you are going to earn just as many that you don't kill.

It is a firm rule that you are going to kill the most turkeys when you don't need any, or worst of all, when you have taken someone with you who hasn't killed one. Or you take a man who needs to kill one badly, and you move heaven and earth to put him in the right place, so that you can call turkeys past him or run turkeys over him.

I have never owned a dead elephant in the summertime, and so speak from no background, but I cannot make myself believe that a dead August elephant is as hard to give away as a wild turkey. Find however many turkeys you can, plan your tactics however carefully you wish, set up the situation as meticulously as you possibly can contrive to give the other man the advantage and the turkey will walk around him and up to you and make you kill him—or if you have left your gun unloaded to make sure you can't kill him, he will run into your leg and break his neck.

I am not implying that turkeys understand these things, or that they have equal intellectual development with men. That would be wholly unjust. A turkey's brain development exceeds that of nearly all vice presidents for instance. And even though he is sometimes capable of abysmal stupidity, he normally reasons on a par with Mycroft Holmes.

There is not any intention on my part to imply that turkey hunting is exactly an even up sport because it is not even close. Bulls do sometimes gore the matador. Charging lions do sometimes maul the hunter. Occupations like these constitute even sports. Turkeys are without fangs or claws or horns and they cannot shoot back. The penalty for losing the game is simply the loss of the turkey, not a reduction in the number of your arms and legs.

But a turkey does have several advantages. He can fly and a man cannot, unaided. His eyesight, especially when it comes to detecting motion, is no less than marvelous, and his hearing simply defies belief. He can hear you yelp at a quarter of a mile, can instantly from that single sound absolutely fix both your direction and your distance and could, if he wanted to, pitch directly from the tree in which he sits and light on your head. He is utterly and wholly suspicious of everything and everybody and unless he is taken over bait or is shot at long range with a rifle has all the cards. Not only does he hold all the good cards, he can read the backs of yours.

In baseball there are people who are called junk pitchers, people without speed, or power, or smoke. Their high hard one comes up to you with the stitches individually visible and all the writing on the ball perfectly readable. If the ball hit you in the Adam's apple it would barely make you cough. But you go 0 for four against people like this day after day, hitting bleeders to second and pop flies to third. They get you off balance when you walk out of the dugout and you don't recover your equilibrium until you have racked your bat and sat down again.

Turkeys do the same thing only they do it infinitely better. Turkeys have an absolute genius for walking up to you on the wrong side and at the wrong time. If there is a single briar patch or blowdown on eighty acres that you cannot see through, they will walk up to you behind it just as surely as if there were no other path through the woods. Not only did turkeys originate Murphy's law, they have rewritten several of its postulates. After what they make go wrong has gone wrong, and then gotten worse, they really get down to work and create trouble.

One of a turkey's principal and less endearing traits is his almost invariable habit of examining things that appear to be the least bit out of the ordinary from a distance. A very long distance.

There are exceptions of course. Very young turkeys often go directly to the yelping. I have seen scattered turkeys fly upwards of two hundred yards to the one old hen who sits in the middle and calls the drove back together. But neither of these are unusual sounds, or are events that seem to a turkey to be anything out of the ordinary.

Normally turkeys will approach one another. One of them does not stand still and call while the other one does all the walking. Even in the spring, when they are concentrating on the girls to the exclusion of everything else, the courtship operates on a dual basis. Despite what tales you may tell about your vanished youth when you were deadly at a thousand yards, you ought to be far too intelligent to tell these stories in the presence of any of the girls you were supposed to be deadly to—you know better. But with turkeys, regardless of how inadequate it may make you feel, a turkey hen will go to a gobbler if anything quicker than a gobbler will go to a hen. A turkey to whom you have yelped in the spring will fly down from the tree when and if he chooses. If he has chosen to fly down in your direction he is only going to come part way. When he gets near what he knows to be the source of the yelping he will usually stop. He will stop here because at this point he knows he is supposed to see a hen. Unlike you and I, no matter what we may say, he clearly knows his worth, and knows from past experience that by now he ought to be able to see the girls on the way. If he does not see them he is going to stop. And most of the time he will remain stopped until he sees something. The longer he stands there without seeing anything the more suspicious he is going to get, and the longer is he going to be inclined to wait there and look over every leaf and twig and bush, millimeter by millimeter. He will simply stand and strut and drum and be attractive, rather than pushy and aggressive, because it has worked so well so many times before.

His ear for the unusual is remarkable. His judgment of what is abnormal is outstanding, and his examination of things he considers to be out of the ordinary he carries on from the maximum distance possible for good observation. I think it is perhaps this meticulous examination of the unusual, coupled with one other thing, that has helped to create much of the legend that surrounds him.

That other thing is an absolute irrationality of behavior that is frequently staggering. He will regularly do things that are so unexpected, so out of context, and so utterly capricious that they defy belief.

To illustrate: A year or two ago, one spring when the river was out of its banks, I was walking slowly along the edge of the backwater late one afternoon. I saw four old gobblers, well out in the swamp, wading around in water an inch or two deep, catching crawfish. I saw them before they saw me—which uses up a month's luck all at once—and lay down behind a stump, and yelped to them without even attracting a glance. After they had moved off along the backwater and had gone out of sight, I got up and ran in a big loop out through the woods in an attempt to get ahead of them. In the maze of flooded sloughs and branches running down into the backwater I became confused, and sat down in the wrong place. It began to get very late before I realized this and realized they had gotten past me, and as darkness approached I heard them flying up to roost, one by one, out over the water. As carefully as possible, I slipped out without disturbing anything and went home. I came back the next morning, and when it got daylight I was already in the woods and was well hidden exactly where I had given up the afternoon before. One of the turkeys gobbled one time on the roost and then pitched down onto a little ridge on my left, a ridge that ran down to the edge of the water, and stood there in the open, no more than ninety yards away.

I yelped to him a couple of times, very softly, and he did look up and exhibit some interest, but then he turned away and began to pick around on the ground. After a long while I yelped again, over my shoulder, like I was somewhere else, and while turning my head slowly back to the front I saw four hens come down along the edge of the water from my right, see the gobbler, and stop directly in front of me at ranges varying from fifteen to forty yards. The gobbler and the four hens were in absolutely plain sight of one another, no more than a hundred yards apart, and with nothing between them but a tiny run of water barely two inches deep and ten feet wide. It was a run I had watched the turkeys wade through the afternoon before, and could not possibly constitute an obstacle.

Those hens, first one, then another, then by twos and threes, and finally all four in unison, began to yelp to that gobbler. I slouched even lower down against my tree, spit out my yelper, got my gun firmly up on my knees, and eased the safety off.

I even decided, partly because I am all heart and partly because I wanted to watch, that I was going to let him, before I shot him.

Those girls, and two of them were good looking, stood there and yelped to that turkey continuously for fifteen minutes. They made offers and suggestions and propositions and promised him things that would have made a Frenchman blush. He listened to all of this very carefully, nodded his head as if he had expected nothing else, firmly turned his back and walked off along the edge of the backwater, eating.

It was absolutely without question the most shocking exhibition of unchivalrous behavior it has ever been my bad luck to encounter. It made you want to weep for all mankind. Any man, or turkey, who would turn down the kind of offers he had just had made to him, and from such a source, on a clear spring morning after a restful night's sleep, must obviously be without the slightest spark of romance and must possess a heart that has shriveled into a cinder.

This was one particular turkey on one particular morning. The very next day, given a similar set of circumstances and only 15 percent as much encouragement another turkey might run three hundred yards to those girls and commit aggravated assault in all directions—or fly seventy-five yards across the water and make love to a pile of holly leaves, spines and all.

You just don't ever know.

It is though, this wide streak of irrationality, this sometimes willful capriciousness, this trait of not only doing the unexpected thing but doing it in the most unexpected ways that makes him so everlastingly interesting. It, beyond all other factors, makes the hunting of him so engrossing, so clearly worth the trouble and keeps you coming back for a fresh slice of humiliation time after time.

Turkeys, of course, make all sorts of noises. Gobblers gobble, loudly or softly at will. Young gobblers will yelp, and squall, and with their voices breaking like those of adolescent boys give forth calls that are part yelp and part gobble and mostly neither. Hens will cluck and putt and yelp and whine. Both sexes will make little chirring noises deep in their throats while they are feeding. I have heard and I have seen turkeys make noises that you would not make in front of people, for fear of being laughed at and embarrassed.

And then there are those "lost chords."

I have had dozens of men lean forward and tell me in the same confidential tones I suspect they would use to reveal the location of the Lost Dutchman Mine, that a turkey hen, while in the act of love, makes a sound that is unlike any other sound she ever utters. They categorically state that if you could ever hear this sound, and learn to imitate it, you would kill so many turkeys that the Fish and Game Department would find it necessary to outlaw you by name, like baited fields and live decoys. They insist that if you could make this sound it would be necessary for you to wear your safety goggles when you hunted, because if you didn't, turkey gobblers would run up and peck your eyes out before you could raise your gun to defend yourself. They imply that it would be dangerous to yelp like this at all, unless you were firmly backed up against a tree before you did it, because if you were not, instant ravishment by sex-crazed gobblers might occur before you could turn around to protect your innocence.

There is also supposed to be a call that turkey hens make

when they are flying down out of the tree, and while they are still in the air, that will bring gobblers from a mile away.

I have never heard any of these calls, although I have listened carefully, nor have I ever met a man who was willing to demonstrate them to me, although some have claimed to know them. But I know they must exist, for the same reason that I know all red-headed girls are passionate and that all Southern pine timber has a form class of 78.

This whole business of calling, and the implied difficulty thereof, has added substantially to the mystique surrounding the hunting of the bird. It has been muddying up the water for a long time too.

Take a look at a collection of the older paintings and illustrations of turkey hunting. A great many of them show the hunter seated in his blind, with his gun presented, and behind him the man doing the calling is dressed as an Indian. The connotation is clear that unless a man had been born in a wigwam or a wickiup, and was teethed on an arrow and a tomahawk handle, he could never possibly master this strangest and darkest of all the arts. Many people believe this, and it is because of this belief that the thick blanket of mystery is spread over calling. Adherence to this belief has been principally responsible for all of those stories about the lost chords.

I know personally, and hunt regularly, with a half dozen men who kill a hell of a lot of turkeys. No two of these individuals yelp alike. All of their yelping sounds as if it were being done by turkeys, of course, but there are wide variations in tone and in pitch, although there is not much variation in timing. At least it seems so to my ear.

No man who uses a mouth yelper can listen to himself properly anyway, without a tape recorder. The sound so resounds from the roof of the mouth, and there is so much vibration in there, that it is about like hearing your own voice. You never really know what that sounds like until you have heard it reproduced.

Hardly any two turkeys yelp alike either, and the range and scope of their sounds are extensive. I have seen a turkey hen stand within gunshot in front of me and imitate every sound I made on a yelper—squeaks, sour notes and all.

The devices, either homemade or sold on the market, that

38

are designed to imitate turkey noises would fill this room. There are cedar and walnut and maple boxes with both fixed and hinged lids. There are snuff cans and wing bones and fragments of slate that come with little sticks to rub across them. There are men who use pieces of switch cane, or pipe stems, or little lead horseshoes with a rubber membrane stretched across the open end. Some hunters use leaves, or blades of grass, or spring-loaded boxes with plungers. I know two or three men who yelp with their vocal cords, unassisted, and do a very presentable job of it, too.

And in all likelihood there are forty or fifty such devices that I am unaware of. Because it is so ancient a tool, there have probably been more turkeys killed with a wing bone than with any other imitative device, but all of these things will kill turkeys. All of them improperly used will make turkeys hurt themselves, laughing.

My own personal opinion is that yelping, or calling if you prefer, is hugely overrated and that it is no more than 30 percent of turkey hunting. I would rank it considerably behind the ability to sit still, and completely out of sight behind the value of knowing the land on which you hunt. By this last I do not mean knowing which counties bound the one you are hunting in, or knowing the road net that gets you from the camp house into the woods. I mean an intimate and exhaustive knowledge of what the land looks like on the other side of the creek, and where the timber types change, and how thick the ground cover is in the next hollow.

A turkey walks about like a man, and he does it in about the same places that a man would walk. He will come out into roads on rainy days, to stay out of the wet bushes, just as you would, and he is no more willing to walk through dense thickets and briar patches than you are. He is generally much more willing to walk straight uphill than a man is and he can fly over obstacles, although he flies over things only as a last resort. A thorough knowledge of the ground gives you the advantage of knowing where a turkey has half a mind to walk anyway, and then if you take the time to hide yourself well and to sit still, you have won nearly half the battle. If your yelping then does not sound like a crow being raped by an eagle and you have taken the trouble to do these other things, it is good enough.

If you find that you cannot accept that statement with both eyebrows in line, take a suggestion. Go to the next turkey calling contest conducted in your town. Go there and listen to some of the outrages perpetrated by men who consider themselves experts, in front of judges who consider themselves to be bigger experts, and watch them get prizes for doing so. Listen to some of the horrible noises made in barber shops and sporting goods stores before the season opens, and better yet, privately and separately approach two or three recognized experts in your region with a tape recorder. Seat yourself intellectually at the feet of these founts of wisdom and humbly ask them to yelp into your machine. Whatever you do, keep your face straight and never smile in a patronizing manner. In fact it is better not to smile at all. Never, never, never comment that you have heard better. Let your entire demeanor be one of awe and praise and flattery. Be as disgustingly humble as you can possibly prostitute yourself into being. Remember back to how you used to act when you chased girls, and hoped to catch them, and act just like that. Remember how you were never so foolish as to comment on how pretty Alice was when you were with Betty, and remember what trouble you got into if you forgot.

After you have done all this, and have gotten two or three experts on the same tape, come home and let the whole thing rest for several days. Then one night after dinner when the house is quiet, go and turn the machine on and listen to all of them carefully, one behind the other. Then do it again—then again. You are going to find exactly one similarity—their timing is going to be very, very close. The pitch will differ, and so will the tone, and so will the number of notes. But the timing between whatever notes they make will be nearly identical. Memorize this timing. Fix it in your mind and quit. Have a nightcap and go to bed. You know enough. You know what has been good enough for a hell of a lot of people to kill a hell of a lot of turkeys for years and years and years.

This mystery about calling, this nearly universal opinion that it is more difficult to master than diamond cutting, this belief that there are two or three sounds which if only a man could learn he would be an instant success, stems from a psychological trait of our society. It is part of our heritage to believe in the shortcut. There is always some pseudo-magical trick that if we could only master we believe we could do anything. Bake better bread, hit curve balls at the knees or always break the bank at Monte Carlo.

This trait of our nature is what causes some preachers to suggest that you rely wholly upon religion. Relax and believe and the Lord will provide. It is what gives some corporation vice presidents their touching and childlike faith in computers, or in any one of a number of consultant-inspired systems of management. The exercise of the intellect becomes secondary or perhaps even tertiary. The Lord, or the computer, or the system will provide. But if you elect to become a member of the Legion you are going to find that ecclesiastically, electronically or psychologically, whatever you may have selected for your deity is not going to provide. You are going to find that you have to work at it, and you are going to have to work at it over a long period of time.

I have not come here to discuss religion, or to discuss the stock market, or to dig into the thought processes of vice presidents, God forbid. I discuss *Meleagris gallopavo* and how to kill him, and my thesis is that yelping is only one small item in your chest of tools. There is no magic solution and there is no gimmick, and there never has been, except for Dixie 18, which you ought not to use.

If you do by any chance have the kind of temperament that demands the magic answer, or if you insist upon guaranteed success, I have a suggestion.

There are all over this end of the country deer hunting clubs that think just like you do and who will be delighted to accept your money. After your election to membership you can get an Abercrombie and Fitch shirt and a pair of sixty-dollar boots and a funny hat and a long knife and fall in. It will rest your head because you won't ever have to use it. You won't use your feet much either and it is likely, as has happened with seals, that they will turn into flippers through disuse.

I cannot leave the subject of the bird himself without a comment on one of the most delightful and appealing aspects of turkey hunting in my area, and that is our feeling for hens.

Hens are not shot in Alabama except through accident. Both Florida and Georgia permit them to be taken in the fall, and privately, I do not think that it does any real harm. You should understand, though, that that statement in Alabama approaches treason. To say those words in public in this state will most surely bring the fury of the hunting community down upon your head.

The furor that accompanied the opening of the doe deer season still rumbles in the background like muted thunderstorms, several years after the fact. Consider the history of that event.

In the face of a population explosion that resulted in grown deer weighing less than ninety pounds, and that caused certain stands of timber to be browsed to the same degree as shade patches in cow pastures, the Conservation Department approached the legislature recommending the opening of a doe season in certain selected counties.

The statewide gap of horror that followed could have only been matched by a suggestion the President-elect of the Alabama Chapter of the Daughters of the Confederacy appear at her investiture both topless and bottomless. The controversy raged for months, both in person and in print.

Finally after repeated appeals and the presentation of pounds of documentary evidence to show that the deer herd was suffering permanent damage, a doe season was opened, although it took an amendment to the state constitution to get it done. It operates very sporadically now in certain selected counties on a doe tag basis. The owner of the land, or the controlling club if the hunting rights are held by other than the owner, is allowed a certain number of doe tags on a seasonal basis, and is supposed to kill that number of does. It is carefully handled by the Department of Conservation, is rigidly controlled, and it ranks in popularity somewhere between the Reconstruction and the Volstead Acts.

There is no question but that the objection is founded not so much on game conservation as it is founded upon chivalry.

Chivalry in Alabama takes various forms, other than the normal ones of saying Ma'am to every female over the age of eleven, and rushing to open doors.

In this state while it is not only possible, but highly likely, for anyone to be awarded a jail sentence for stealing hogs, it is almost impossible for a lady to suffer any but the most minor of inconveniences if she has to shoot her husband.

There are certain ground rules, of course. Husband shooting should be done with a handgun, and it ought to be done at home. Preferably it should take only one shot, although in certain cases two are permissible. If the lady will follow certain broad guidelines, Alabama lawyers can establish a marvelous rapport with juries and have exhibited a remarkable ability to win acquittals.

The lady should appear in court in dark, loosely fitting clothes. She must appear two or three days in succession in the same outfit, freshly washed and pressed, thereby giving the impression of genteelly straightened financial circumstances.

Her attorneys will then gently allude to the unwritten law, firmly implant in the minds of the jury that the brute quite obviously deserved it, and with the not always silent approval of the bench, the jury will quite often acquit without ever leaving the box. The rules of chivalry forbid that our fragile flowers be put through the mental anguish of waiting for the jury to go out, simply so they can turn around and come back to render a verdict of not guilty.

Unfortunately, a jury will occasionally bend this rule if the lawyers have been so crude and unfeeling as to let the case go to the jury just before suppertime. Juries, being composed largely of loutish husbands, feel that they are entitled to a meal on the county, and will sometimes prolong their deliberations long enough to eat before rushing back into the box to turn the poor innocent creature loose.

Understand that I am finding no fault with this state of affairs. Being a husband myself, I know that we are all brutes, agree that justice must always be served and consider chivalry to be one of the few genuinely unselfish emotions that we have.

In passing, I think the ladies have made a serious tactical error in the last few years by insinuating themselves into jury boxes. Why they have insisted upon doing it, I have no idea, for they can only have done themselves harm. Attorneys nowadays must go to the time and the trouble to challenge and pettifogg and find cause until they have managed to select an all-male jury in these husband accident cases, which introduces a difficulty into the affair that is unnecessary. I think that the ladies are handicapping themselves unfairly.

Since half the turkey hens in a given hatch are going to die from natural causes during their first year anyhow, no real harm could come from killing some of them in the fall.

Any Director of Conservation who seriously proposed that they be shot, would be violating one of our oldest and most basic of folkways, and would be in real jeopardy of suffering the same fate himself.

He ought to suffer it. Proper game management practices notwithstanding, it would be as unchivalrous to shoot hens as it would be to put ladies in jail for such minor peccadillos as shooting husbands.

In cultivated societies there are certain things that simply are not done.

5

PLACES

The upper coastal plain is a very special place, and fall is a very special time. A hundred miles north of the coast there is a dividing line across the state that is as definite as the seashore. This boundary marks the upper limit of the lower coastal plain and signifies the end of the longleaf, slash and gallberry types common to the lower section. The country grows steeper, and rolling hills and steep hollows become more common. The line is as definite and plain a boundary as a seashore because that is what it used to be. Several geological eras ago, before the lower plain rose up out of the sea, this was the coast. All across upper Conecuh, Monroe, Wilcox, Clarke and Choctaw counties, it is possible to find fossilized oyster shells imbedded in lime rock on the tops of ridges a hundred feet above the creek floor.

The line of transition is so abrupt and so definite that in many cases a road distance of half a mile is sufficient to put you definitely out of one land type and into the other. In Monroe County, for instance, it changes over wholly within the city limits of the county seat, Monroeville, the south city limits sign of which is in typical gallberry flats, and the north limit sign in cove hardwood. The paucity of species of trees and shrubs in the lower plain changes, and a rich variety of hardwoods mingled in with pines occurs.

There are fifteen or twenty species of oaks alone. There is hickory and poplar, beech and ash and elm, maple and gum—

the list goes on and on through ten chapters in the dendrology text. There is just as sharp a change in the understory, too, a change from bunch grass, gallberry and dwarf post oak, to small mixed hardwoods and shrubs. The most remarkable change of all occurs in the creek bottoms.

Creek bottoms in old growth longleaf types in the coastal flats were supposed to be like parks. After hearing old woods rats talk about them for years, I finally found one and they were right. They did look like that seventy-five years ago. You could really shoot woodcock at thirty yards along the run of the creek itself. But they don't look like that anymore. Creek bottoms in today's normal second and third growth lower coastal plain are a vegetative slum. There is bay and blackgum, all of which is crooked and most of which is scrubby. There is on occasion some good slash pine, but the ground is mud, and the whole area is understoried with titi and laced together with smilax vines. It is either hot and wet or cold and flooded. It is difficult to cross, hell to log and thickly populated with cottonmouth moccasins. To a lower coastal plain logger or timber cruiser, the word creek is, with rare exceptions, a dirty word. A four letter word with five letters.

Cross over into the upper plain, though, and the scene changes. Creeks have steep banks with a four- or five-foot drop down to the water. There is occasional rock in the bed of the creek itself and the banks are firm. The timber is mostly mixed hardwoods with patches of loblolly and spruce—spruce pine, that is, not spruce spruce. The understory is generally light except for some mountain laurel thickets.

I can't really say why I despise titi and tolerate mountain laurel. It is surely not the flower; it is not there long enough. Both are junk species, both make thickets that preclude the growth of anything else, both have twisted boles and low growth. But the one offends me and the other does not, even in tangles of equal thickness.

At any rate, creek bottoms up here become places of pleasure and not pest holes. The entire aspect of the land and of the timber changes as you cross the dividing line almost to the degree that you see in altitude species changes in mountain timber. It is hill country.

Hill country after the first frost is a world apart. In dry

years, the leaves of the beech and the hickory and some of the oaks turn scarlet and orange and bright yellow before they fall. There is one hard maple here, called strangely enough Florida maple, whose leaves turn the clearest, palest yellow imaginable. It is a very small tree, nearly a bush, and constitutes a middle story. The sunlight striking down through these layers of color turns the very air golden. I don't believe I have been as drunk on good bourbon as I have gotten on crisp December air. And the color lasts a good while too. Most years the leaves are not all gone until Christmas.

From the tops of ridges you can see successive rows of ridges, the mixed pine turning from green to bluer green and ultimately at the final horizon into a hazy blue. If the land is quite hilly, the pine is largely restricted to the ridge tops, and the side hills and lower slopes and creek bottoms are mostly hardwood. The prime hardwood that grew along the creeks was all cut years ago, but heavy stands of second-class timber remain. Along rocky slopes and at the heads of small hollows the timber is mostly big, but there it is largely defective. Repeated woods fires in past years have caused scars, which allowed the butt rot to enter the trunk and create cull trees. These have been left uncut. Beech especially, turns defective quickly, and occurs in almost pure stands sometimes ten acres in size. Since the ground is too steep for conversion to pine, landowners have been forced to accept those species that normally occur, and the steep terrain has made logging expensive. As a consequence, vast acreages are covered with a timber type, that except for the size of the trees, looks about as it did when there was only one road from Montgomery to the Gulf, and when it was owned in fee by George III—and in fact by his tenants in place, the Creek Nation.

A beech hollow, at three o'clock on a crisp November afternoon, may be the stillest place on earth. After we have a cold front here, we usually have two days of blustery north wind. Before the wind flow begins again from the south, while we are still under the dome of high pressure, there is a day or two that is breathless and the sky is a limitless blue.

Like so many other people I rent out my days for money. Normally I can accept my fate with equanimity, but on afternoons like this rebellion bubbles very near the surface and sometimes it boils over.

The timber in these beech hollows is usually big—it develops butt rot early and was left in the first logging, and though beech is highly tolerant, it will have cleaned itself of lower limbs up to a height of fifty feet or so. The ground too, is clean—because of the heavy beech shade in the growing season. Early in the fall, with the sun coming through the yellow leaves, there is the same golden wash in the air that you see in the background of a good water color. The trunks of the beech are a light gray, with mottled irregular splotches of greenish gray, and are smooth. Later in the year, after the leaves go, the sunlight comes in more strongly and the background wash, because of the sky, is blue rather than yellow. The hot yellows and oranges then turn to muted grays and soft browns and gray blacks, and all the colors are quieter. The woods appear infinitely more open and distances seem shorter—the other side of the hollow seems to be closer than it really is.

Very late in the afternoon when the squirrels begin to bark and move around and the birds begin to scuffle in the leaves it is reasonably noisy. But there is a period an hour or so before when the hush is utter, and the silence absolute. There is something about three hours alone in here without the sound of another human voice that is restorative. If the same three hours can be spent out of the sight of another human face, the pleasure is at least doubled.

It is an aloneness that is wholly free from loneliness even though as you enjoy it you are in a sense fooling yourself. You are not the last man on earth nor do you honestly want to be. It is really difficult nowadays to get more than five or six miles from somebody's house—air miles—and you hardly ever get more than a mile or two from the car. But to achieve a feeling that is so remarkably pleasant it really does not do any harm to fool yourself a little bit. I have never minded anybody lying to me if it made me feel good.

Make no mistake but that the purpose in hunting turkeys is to kill some, not to worship nature. Hill country turkeys, though, have the principal added advantage in that they live in such delightful places that simply being able to visit their ground is a pleasure.

I am aware too that I am doubly fortunate. As a young man I was able to make a living in places like this and so was able to develop a taste for them. And it is quite positively an acquired taste. There is a vast difference between making a living in the woods and hunting in them on crisp November afternoons. When you work, it is not always November, sometimes it is August. Then it rains often. Then it is hot and green and sticky. Then there are blackberry briars and smilax vines, and there are deer flies and red bugs and ticks and mosquitoes. After hurricanes in the summer, there is a species of mosquito, locally called a gallinipper, that is a dandy. He can quite easily sting you through a pair of brand new khaki pants, if they are pulled tight over the skin at the thigh or the butt, and he does it all the time. There are snakes. Rattlesnakes, both the diamondback and the big one, the Florida diamondback, plenty of cottonmouths, some copperheads, and even a few coral snakes. None of these are conducive to a contemplative enjoyment of your surroundings. Working here has another principal disadvantage. Hunters and timber markers can both walk around obstacles, hunters more than markers, of course. Markers have to go to every tree, hunters don't have to go anywhere. Timber cruisers, because of the demands of their job, must necessarily walk in straight lines and this can create a wretched state of affairs sometimes.

I once possessed a compass that did not point to the magnetic pole, but rather sought out with unerring accuracy briar patches, never less than a half acre in diameter. There is nothing like finding one of these patches of waist-high briars, late in the afternoon when you are good and tired, and you came to work that morning wearing your thinnest pants for coolness. Briar patches are what make the front of timber cruiser's legs look as if they had been wading through mad, wet cats.

Like everything else, though, as you get a little older you forget the bad parts and remember only the good, and going back now that you don't have to, on selected delightful days, is like a return to your young manhood. You get a little more tired than you used to get, late in the afternoon, but there is a simple explanation for this.

While there seems to be no official record of geologic upheavals in South Alabama in the last twenty-five years, how

49

they could have possibly gone unnoticed is beyond my comprehension. There must have been dozens. I know there have been because there are dozens of hills that to my positive knowledge are immensely steeper than they were twenty-five years ago. They are higher than they were, as well as steeper. The air on top of them is considerably thinner than it used to be after you get up there and you have to breathe a lot more of it than you did the old-time, thick, solid air to get the same amount of good out of it—and you have to breathe it a lot quicker too.

But the smell of the hills is the same, and the feel of them is the same, and the ground falls away under your feet just like it used to. Creek water is just as cold, and beechnuts taste just as sweet, and your appreciation of the hush and the color and the solitude is not lessened by the passage of the years, I believe rather that it is heightened.

Strangely enough there are not a whole hell of a lot of people who work in the woods who hunt. There are a lot of men who work there, and when there is no work to do in the woods, stay out of them. Of course it is not really common to see a man take his pleasure where he works, no matter what his job. The piano player always goes to bed in a different house. If you hunt, you don't take the pleasure in the same way, although you do take it on the same ground. It is often very difficult to explain, but people who work in the woods are working. A man may be cruising, or marking, he may be laying out roads, he may be looking over a logging chance, but it is a job and he is working at it. Trees at this point are not vegetative sculpture, but products—objects of commerce. Hills and creeks are not charming terrain irregularities but are obstacles that must be surmounted before the objects of commerce can be counted or measured or extracted.

You can go early and hunt before you work. You can quit early and hunt after you quit. But you cannot hunt and work at the same time and do either one of them with any degree of competence. You look at the same things with such different eyes, depending upon your purpose for being there.

It depends upon the situation and the purpose and your point of view. Old growth beech and bird-pecked hickory and fire-scarred hill oak is simply defective junk when you consider logging it. It becomes an outstanding example of climax forest when you come to hunt in it.

I am not trying to make a religious cult out of all this; my Mama was never frightened by the Druids. There are dozens and dozens of men who hunt competently and with perfect enjoyment who couldn't tell a white oak from a yellow poplar if either one fell on them. Hunting turkeys has never required a technical background in dendrology. But the pursuit of any game bird or animal depends quite a lot on atmosphere. If turkeys were jump shot out of marsh grass, like snipe, I would have given it up some years ago, or perhaps not even started.

I have killed some turkeys on the edges of pastures and I have killed some in pine thickets. I hope to kill a lot more in both places. But I would rather hunt one and not kill him, under old growth beech and hickory on steep ground, than I would to jump him out of a gallberry head and shoot him. It just somehow seems proper to find him in the one place and not proper to find him in the other.

Many people, you see, have a real feeling for timber, especially and even people like me who have been responsible for cutting down and using a good many millions of board feet of it. From my standpoint the feeling of the pure enjoyment of timber depends upon the presence or absence of understory. We ought to talk a little bit about understory.

The first year I was out of school I marked timber for an old line Southern lumber company. It can perhaps do no harm to explain that a timber marker is a man who goes out before the logging crew and selects, by marking with paint, the trees to be cut. He works alone, day after day all day long, gets to know the country foot by foot, and has ample time to use his head to compose sonnets, which is fortunate, because after he learns his job his head is at rest, he has no further use for it and there is nothing else to do with it. It is a job given mostly to young men with strong legs. If these young men have active intellects as well, it is a marked disadvantage. If you choose to follow this profession though, it will do one of two things for you. You will either develop a lasting appreciation of timber and silence and solitude or you will go gently mad. And you can go either way with equal facility. Some of my friends still sometimes ask me which way I went.

The company I worked for owned a tract of some 50,000 acres separated by a distance of sixty miles from the balance of their holdings. Large parts of this separate tract had had an unusual history. Because of a peculiar combination of depressions and a change in logging systems between the two World Wars—it was bought in 1914—there remained uncut some two or three thousand acres of old growth longleaf pine. A lot of this virgin timber was in scattered eighties and quarter sections, and because fire protection in the upper coastal plain is so much easier than it is in the wiregrass farther south, this acreage had not burned over since the purchase.

Old growth longleaf pine, three hundred years of age and older, does not stand many trees to the acre. The timber in this stand was absolutely magnificent. Trees thirty inches in diameter were not common on the tally book, but they were not uncommon either. You marked one, mentally said "good tree," and kept working. Volumes ran ten thousand feet to the acre, but when you are averaging five hundred feet a tree it does not take many trees to stock an acre.

The understory was a jungle. Hill blackgum and dwarf post oak, laced together by smilax vines with the thorns freshly sharpened. Wax myrtle and persimmon and yaupon and God alone knows how many species of Craetaegus, whose thorns had been sharpened the day after the smilax. The whole unpleasant mess was underlain with tangles and blowdowns and briars and jasmine vines nearly knee-deep, and visibility was limited to fifteen yards. It was without question the finest timber I ever worked in, so far as size and grade and quality were concerned, and the most unimpressive and the most damnably miserable to move around in.

The forest primeval, despite the yearning panegyrics of necktie salesmen and ladies' garden clubs, neither of whom ever saw any, is quite often a pain in the ass—or to be utterly accurate, a thorn rather than a pain.

The secret is the canopy. Canopy is an inside word for the closure effected by the branches of the tree. When the branches interlace with the branches of adjoining trees the canopy is considered closed.

Canopy closure is what largely limits the understory because of the denial of sunlight to the forest floor, although soil fertility does have an effect as well.

Old growth longleaf on sand ridges, even at ten trees per acre, grows over a grass floor and is a park. It is a park even under a partial canopy because of the infertility of the soil. In the upper coastal plain, because of the relative richness of the soil, even on the tops of ridges, old growth timber, unless the canopy is closed, will turn out to be eight thousand feet of prime sawlogs per acre growing in a brush pile. Decked out on a landing already made into logs, it is impressive. Standing on the stump it is an esthetic failure.

Close the canopy though, and whether you close it with forty-year-old oak, or with mixed pine and hardwood, or with ancient defective beech and hickory, the understory melts away. Visibility increases to two hundred yards or better, and the boles of the trees do, in fact, become the supporting pillars of the roof of the cathedral—to fall back on the metaphor so beloved by nature magazines. This is what sets up the situation of a parklike interior, the situation that during the early winter with the leaves gone and the sunlight streaming down onto the clean leaf floor, brings to mind Mark Twain's deathless line. The one about steamboat races. The one that says it is an experience "to make a body's very liver curl with enjoyment."

Human populations of one or two at a time in these places can be pleasant. The gathering of gangs of people, whether for a hunt or a birdwalk or a mushroom picking is absolutely unsuitable.

There is another side to it.

What little winter we do get here comes in streaks. It will cloud up and rain for two or three days, with a south wind. Then on the third or fourth day the wind shifts into the northwest and it turns progressively colder all day long while the rain continues. While it is still raining, the very places that will be so delightful in two days or that were so pleasant the day before yesterday become sketches from Dante, painted with a dirty brush. The rain comes down in a fierce and penetrating drizzle. You and everything in the world become cold and dank and sodden. The leaf mold holds water in unimaginable gallons, and with every step the water that is inside and under your boots squishes. Water always gets in your boots. If it doesn't come in through the holes, it runs down into the tops from your wet pants legs. You feel as if you are walking on wet sponges. There is no possible combination of foul weather clothing you can wear that can keep the water from trickling down the back of your neck. The metal parts of your gun have a peculiar cold clamminess under your hand and the gun gets slippery. Everything drips. Beech bark, which is normally a light gray green, becomes a dark slimy gray. Oak bark turns to a nasty black. The branches in the canopy, instead of reaching up into a limitless blue and white sky and tossing, no longer sway, they writhe—against a dirty gray background.

Your thought processes now run mainly to funerals and suicides and bankruptcy courts. You operate with your psychological tail tucked wetly between your legs in a climate not of enjoyable aloneness but of spooky loneliness. You feel as if you were playing hide and seek, and you hid, and nobody came to look for you. It is the kind of day good only to sit upon the ground and "tell sad stories about the deaths of kings."

You ought to have a day such as this every once in a while though. It helps to keep you from feeling too sure of yourself.

Turkeys are hunted on days like this, just as they are hunted on golden days, and they are also hunted in other terrain.

I do not really think I speak too much of terrain. The hunting of turkeys is so equally intermeshed with the bird, the people who do it, and the ground they do it on, that it all comprises a whole and cannot conveniently be separated.

Although we have so far been concentrating upon hill country, there is one other principal turkey range in the Southeast, a range that holds as many, or more, turkeys as uplands, and has held them longer. It was really the only area that had them in any numbers during the dark ages. This is the river swamp.

The word swamp here is really a misnomer. Swamp is what you used to see in the 1937 movies, with the whole cast wading knee-deep in water, and all the natives carrying bundles on their heads. Everybody had a machete, except the female lead, and were busily chopping snakey looking vines and lianas in all directions.

What is called river swamp down here is the bottom land

along the major rivers. It is always in one of two conditions—delightful or impossible.

Normally in January the wet season begins. The major river systems begin to rise then, come out of the banks, and quickly get to the winter stages and stay there until March. This is the impossible season, and it is impossible because most of the swamp is under four feet of water. It is not an area in which to hunt turkeys or anything else; it is the bottom of a lake.

In the fall, before the floods, and in the spring after they have gone, the land along the river bottoms is delightful.

The river gets back into its banks then and stays there, where it belongs. At low stages there is a four- to six-foot bank for miles and miles. It is perfectly flat in the woods along the river, a ridge a foot high being an event, and three is no pine. Very occasionally as you get seventy-five miles above the delta, there are single spruce pines, but primarily it is a world of hardwood. A staggering variety of hardwoods—and of superior form and growth, too. I have seen persimmon trees growing in river swamps that would make class 4/40 poles, and if you will recall the normal, scrubby, half-bush persimmons you see along fence rows, you will realize the difference in the tree depending upon the soil in which it grows. There is a species of oak that grows in river bottoms, cherry bark oak, that will often be fourteen inches in diameter, a hundred feet tall, and will be shaped like a longleaf pine sixty years old.

In good years—one in every three or four—the volume of acorns produced in river swamps defies belief. Year before last we had one of those good mast years, and during the month of November it was not possible to put your hand on the ground anywhere and not touch an acorn. Turkeys not only did not find it necessary to scratch, they could lay down and stretch their necks and fill up.

After these lowlands are first logged the bushes and briars make positive jungles, but the growth is so fast, and the canopy closes so quickly that the bottom rapidly reverts to its former aspect. And its most pronounced aspect is its visibility. There are quite literally thousands of acres so flat and so clear of underbrush that it would be perfectly possible to shoot a man four hundred yards away with a rifle, unless he was standing behind a tree.

This flatness and cleanliness causes an outstanding characteristic—a humiliating one—of hunting in river swamps, and honesty compels me to discuss it.

For years I hunted without a compass. Compasses, I felt, were an item of equipment only necessary for ribbon clerks, people who got into the woods in alternate Novembers. Most modern compasses are made now with the east and west directions reversed and with a mirror inside a hinged lid. The mirror is used to see the needle when you take a sight, and the mirror image straightens out the direction. I can remember saying to anybody who would listen that the principal value in such a compass was this mirror. After it had happened, you could take out the compass and open it up and use the mirror to see who was lost.

Professionals like me, I used to say, used compasses to run boundary lines or to cruise timber—not to hunt. I used to go even further and say in calm, irritating tones, that I would begin to carry a compass the day I started carrying a cane.

Like so many other words that I have eaten, these very syllables scratched all the way down.

A winter day, with no wind, and no sun, and one of those light misty drizzles in a river swamp will turn your head around in a minute. Everything looks exactly the same in every direction. You can walk in straight lines and come out eventually, but it is somewhat less embarrassing to go on and bite the bullet and carry your compass to begin with. I carry one now all the time, and I carry it without a cane either.

Spring turkeys are hunted about the same in the swamp as in the hills. Fall turkeys are infinitely more difficult in there because of the lack of understory. They can see you so far off, so long before you see them, that it adds substantially to the difficulty.

And no matter what you may have heard about fall turkey hunting, it does really have a difficulty or two. It is honestly not necessary to walk along ringing a bell and shouting "Unclean, unclean," so as not to take unfair advantage of the poor little things.

6

FALL

Fall turkey hunting can perhaps best be described as lively, and is characterized by noise and motion and lots of excitement. Until turkeys are found and scattered there is a great deal of walking involved. A man really ought to start to learn turkey hunting in the fall. It will have a tendency to cure him of a great deal of the tippy-toe attitude that is normal with beginning turkey hunters. He will hear so many in the fall, and see so many, that the sense of awe about turkeys that occasionally arises in the spring can be stifled. A turkey is, after all, only a bird. In the spring, because he looms so much larger than life, it becomes easy to overestimate him, and you can overestimate him but you should not deify him. You are going to have ample trouble in your dealings with him without assigning attributes to him that he does not really possess. Fall humanizes him and lets you see him in what is really a state that is closer to his proper perspective.

Fall turkeys, being still in droves as they are at this time of the year, will yelp some on the roost at daylight. Each one seems to want to be sure where the other is before he flies down, as if he had forgotten overnight. After they have flown down, and for a period of perhaps half an hour, they yelp a lot. If the drove is large, or as happens in cases of extremely high populations, is composed of a dozen or so young gobblers, the amount of noise they will make then is perfectly scandalous.

Turkeys will stand ten feet apart and squall at one another.

They will run about and chase each other, screaming all the time, like school children at recess. Gobbler fights break out all round, complete with lunging and leaping and flying together accompanied by wing flapping and spurring and pecking. Except for the pecking, it reminds you of nothing quite so much as a Christmas party where everyone came in a festive mood to begin with, and the dinner has been unavoidably delayed for an hour. This then extends the cocktail hour far beyond the normal decent interval and finally there are fourteen conversations going on simultaneously, nobody is listening but everybody is talking, and the decibel count has gotten way up into the earplug level.

Turkeys will often mill around and yell at one another like this for the better part of an hour before they begin to simmer down; and only after they have gotten this out of their systems do they begin to move off. As they move they feed, and the forward motion of the group is at about the same speed as a man would saunter, if he were in no particular hurry to get anywhere and was simply walking along breathing the air and looking at the timber. In timber types that run heavily to hardwood, turkeys leave a lot of sign. Through areas that have been traversed by big droves the amount of sign left in the leaves is striking. Leaves are left in windrows and in piles and there are enough places with the mineral soil exposed so that you can often walk a hundred yards and put your feet on nothing but the bare ground.

If you hear them when they first begin to yelp at daylight and move quickly, you may be able to get to them soon enough to scatter them off the roost. If you are a little later, and don't hear them until they are in the throes of the early morning hell-raising period, right after they fly down, you may still be able to get to them then. If all this racket is going on down in a steep hollow you may be lucky enough to get to a point above them. Then you can run quickly to the edge of the hollow and shoot down into it. This does two things. It seems to magnify the noise your gunshot makes, which is a help, and the appearance of something above turkeys seems to trigger some atavistic fear (they may remember eagles or something) and it really moves them.

The sight and sound of thirty or forty turkeys boiling out of

58

a hollow under your feet, flying straight up or fanning out like a covey of tremendous quail, is nothing less than soul stirring. It appeals as does nothing else to my primitive barbaric soul.

This business of scattering turkeys gives rise to several schools of thought, as you would imagine. And, as you probably likewise imagine, I have some very firm thoughts of my own on the matter. All of these thoughts can be summed up in one sentence.

I think that more turkeys are not killed in the fall because they were improperly scattered than for any other reason.

You can kill fewer by staying home, or by going to play golf, or by not loading your gun, but those are about the only things I can think of that will let you kill less than partially scattering turkeys.

To use another sentence or two and make it even stronger, I do not think it is possible for you to overscatter them. You might be able to do it with a Battalion of 155's and an unlimited ammunition supply rate but you sure as hell can't do it with one or two men armed with shotguns.

Turkeys that have flown off, not scattered mind you, but simply flown, are going to do one thing. They will all fly off in one direction like a covey of quail, light in trees thirty yards or so apart, and wait. Shortly afterward they will begin to cluck back and forth to one another, pitch out, partially gather together while on the way down, light, fluff their wings, and begin to feed. They will be in little groups of two or three almost immediately, and 90 percent of the drove will be firmly reunited in less than two hours. There may still be little groups of three or four running around separately but you are whipped. You can sit around in there and yelp until the roof of your mouth gets sore to no purpose. Some of these little groups will answer you back all day long every time you yelp but you cannot eat answers—answers weigh about as much as turkey tracks. You will leave the woods, suitably chastened, at dark, having been yelped at all day long and with a large, juicy slice of fresh air and sunshine for your trouble. You can carry this trophy home wrapped up in your ill temper. You will have ample material to wrap it up in.

If you do try to scatter turkeys, not shoo them now, but honestly scatter them, you are going to have to shoot to do it, and you are probably going to want to shoot more than once. If you think you did an inferior job of the initial contact and walk in the direction most of them took when they flew, it is generally wise, as you push singles and doubles and triples out of trees, to shoot a little more. It won't hurt anything and it is likely to help tremendously.

I ought to make it perfectly clear here that I am not discussing shooting at turkeys, I am discussing shooting in the direction of turkeys. In nearly all cases they will be firmly out of range of the shot, but you don't care about that at this point. What you want is noise, and they can hear you shoot. Turkeys not shot toward will generally just run off on the ground. Shooting gets them up, makes them fly, and is almost the only way you have of splitting them up. It also serves to firmly establish in their minds which side you are on, and impresses upon them the seriousness of the situation.

The single disadvantage it has that I can think of, is that in this affluent age magnum shotgun shells cost eighteen cents each.

Quite often very large droves of turkeys are extremely difficult to scatter. It can be done off the roost at daylight with some success, or done at dark with about the same degree of competence. But they roost over a surprisingly large area and you will leave some still in the trees in either instance. In the middle of the day though, they are strung out over such a hell of a distance on the ground while they are feeding, that while you are shooting over one end of the drove the other end is running off on the ground. You will see turkeys getting up, and you will hear turkeys running, and you will fool yourself into thinking you have done a lot of good when all you have really done is to have performed in a remarkably inferior manner. They will end up gathered into those nasty little groups that walk around and yelp back at you all the time, and never come, and shrivel your id with frustration.

Turkeys scattered the previous evening will be yelping at daylight. Scattered off the roost at daylight, or off the ground later in the day, they are much slower to begin. It may take an hour or so for them to settle down after either of the last two situations. They have not had all night to sit around in and think about it and get lonesome.

In all three cases the emotion to which you must appeal is gregariousness. Sex we must leave till later in the discussion. For sex, with turkeys, happens only in the spring.

In any event, at any time of the day, at any time in the fall, turkeys that have been exposed to dogs are hopeless.

Before you rise in righteous wrath to stone me, you should understand that I like dogs. For years I kept bird dogs—by the penful. I had dogs in the house, dogs in the yard and dogs in the kitchen. No fireplace even yet, and I have one, do I consider complete without a house dog lying in front of it, in the way— tripping you up when you go to get more wood and jumping up howling when you poke the fire and cause the sparks to fly out and sting him.

The same fire cannot be properly enjoyed as you sit in front of it unless there is a dog's chin on your knee. There is something incomplete about it, like listening to Tchaikovsky's Sixth with one ear.

But dogs in conjunction with turkeys are like cobras and mongoose, or mongeese, whatever the plural happens to be.

Let me illustrate.

In our end of the state the major river swamps are fine turkey range. These areas had turkeys back in the dark ages when almost no place else had them. In the spring, river swamp turkeys act like turkeys are supposed to act. They gobble correctly, they yelp sensibly, they are as normal and predictable as turkeys ever let themselves get, and you feel comfortable and at home in dealing with them and getting fooled by them. But this is not so in the fall, and it is not so for one principal reason—dogs.

Virtually all river bottom land is controlled by hunting clubs. The overwhelming majority of these clubs are associations of deer hunters. During the fall, when the deer and turkey seasons coincide, nearly all of these clubs have weekly hunts. Bi-weekly at the very least. As is normal with most members of the tribe they hunt deer in formal drives on Saturday and Sunday and then hunt lost dogs until the following Thursday. They miss more dogs than they do deer, and as a consequence, from the 15th of November until the 1st of February the woods are full of dogs all the time.

Beginning at a point fifty miles above the confluence of the

Alabama and the Tombigbee rivers, and from there south to the marsh grass in the delta, any morning you care to go out, or any afternoon for that matter, you are seldom out of the sound of dogs.

It almost makes a man want to keep cats.

Since 1710 there has been a regrettable and wholly unjustifiable tendency among the inhabitants of our seacoast to patronize inlanders. Upcountry people have been, not always secretly, considered to be uncultivated, semi-barbaric hill tribes—intellectually barefooted as it were. This reasoning has never had much basis in fact, and in recent years it has grown to have even less.

These people are far too cultivated to run deer with dogs for one thing, in spite of unjustifiable and misplaced flatland snobbery.

At any rate turkeys who are exposed to continuous waves of dogs throughout the deer season will fall silent. After the first two weeks of the deer season you will begin to flush single turkeys out of trees at ten-thirty in the morning, or even at two o'clock in the afternoon. Turkeys will yelp once or twice on the roost in the morning, in tones inaudible at fifty yards, and shut up for the balance of the day. They will not leave, they will simply adapt. And their adaptation in this case takes the form of imitating the vocal characteristics of an Egyptian mummy.

A year or two ago I took a week's vacation in the fall. It fell during a week when the weather was good, an event remarkable in itself. The frost that year had been early, most of the leaves were fallen, and the year's acorn crop was superior. I remember too that we were under the influence of a mass of Canadian high pressure, and day after day dawned crisp and clear and windless. It was dry enough to hear a turkey walk, half a quarter away.

The area I hunted in was full of turkeys and I knew the terrain thoroughly, but it was also full of dogs. I scattered turkeys off the roost on three consecutive mornings at daylight, and scattered them well—scattered them over half a section. And on three consecutive days I left the woods at noon without hearing another sound.

I am not so naive as to suppose that turkeys are obliged to come when I call to them. Nor am I so unintelligent as to expect them to answer every time I yelp, but they are supposed to answer one another. And these turkeys didn't. They never do in such a situation.

Dog-harried turkeys will make the angels weep.

River swamp turkeys, as exceptionally difficult as they are to scatter even under the very best of circumstances, become, when scattered, an event. Three successive droves, scattered on three successive mornings, is almost the millennium. You are going to do this only upon the rarest of rare occasions. And if you are fortunate enough to do it at all, you deserve a better fate than six hours of silence. With turkeys there is no obligation on their part to give you what you deserve, but you really ought to get it every once in a while.

Hill country turkeys, God bless 'em, not only live and operate in areas with somewhat thicker understory but you can take advantage of folds in the ground or ridges to make your final approach. Upon occasion, if you are very careful, and at the last, very quick, you will be able to get close enough to be able to kill one in the drove when you scatter them. I have never kept score on this, but if memory serves me correctly, it will work out to about one killed this way for every seven or eight droves you scatter. Here again as is normal in fall hunting, the uncertainty is responsible for a great deal of the fascination, and you are going to be afforded some marvelous opportunities to out-think yourself. I will not attempt to cover all the possibilities. I cannot think of them all. But an example or two will serve.

Assume that you walk out on the point of a ridge one crisp fall afternoon, stop to enjoy the air for a minute, and then yelp down into one of the hollows on either side of you. I, as an aside, have a childlike faith about yelping down hollows. Hollows always seem to me to be places of mystery and of pleasant anticipation. I always expect the most unexpected and delightful things to come up out of hollows. I never pass one without yelping down into it, even if I am on the way out of the woods and am within a hundred yards of the car. But assume that in this hypothetical instance and overlooking this hypothetical hollow you have yelped one time and you are immediately answered.

This answer opens the action, and you are now faced with

an almost unlimited number of possibilities each simultaneously requiring a decision.

The answer could have come from a single turkey who has become separated from his drove for any one of a number of reasons. It could have come from a turkey still in the tree, who was part of a drove that was scattered earlier in the day by foxes, dogs, squirrel hunters, wildcats or any one of a number of several natural causes. It could have come from one of a group of three or four turkeys in a drove that has partway completed the process of reassembly. It could have come from a turkey in an intact drove who thinks you are lost and who is trying to call you to him. It could, as sometimes happens, have come from another turkey hunter. Any one of these things is just as possible as is any other, at this point you are sure of nothing, and each one of them requires a different course of action.

Normally if you have hunted for any length of time with a man, you have come to know what his yelping sounds like, and no matter how good it is, it is familiar to you. Usually if there are two of you, you have begun operations by going in different directions, in order to cover twice as much ground and double your chances of finding something. But sometimes you have gotten back closer together than you think, and often your imagination plays tricks on you and moves you to the wrong conclusion.

Invariably though, unless you are convinced it is another man, you are going to hide quickly and yelp a little more. You have to—it is the only sensible means you have of clarifying the situation. It is the only way you can reduce the number of possibilities facing you. In a great many cases you will yelp now and be answered again.

If you are answered, while it usually clears up the question of whether or not it is a man, it opens up several other avenues of thought, and requires another decision.

If it is a single turkey and he is coming toward you, and you don't sit still, you are going to run him off. If you do sit still, and rather than a single turkey it is an intact drove, you have the dim possibility of calling up the whole drove, although I can't scrape up a hell of a lot of confidence in anybody calling up whole droves of turkeys on any kind of a regular basis. Sometimes you do, but I think really that what you have done is that you have altered their course somewhat—bent them a little from the direction they intended to go in anyhow. If you sit still too long, and it is an intact drove, they can just as easily be going in the opposite direction and can walk out of hearing, and you can lose contact with them and not regain it for the balance of the day. This last is a real possibility if it is early in the year and they have not yet scratched much and have left little sign.

You may hear a third answer, or you may not. You may not even get a second answer. You may call up a single turkey. You may find that it is a whole drove and have an opportunity to scatter them from where you sit. It could be a whole drove and you may have an opportunity to get above them, or you may have a chance to get up and get around them, or you may have to run a hundred yards into the back end of them and shoot to make them fly as they begin to run off. But the whole process, the entire situation, from the time you are first answered until you scatter them, or lose them, or run them off, is normally a series of decisions which you are going to have to make very rapidly and execute instantaneously after you have made them. It is an exercise of the intellect far more than it is an exercise of the feet, and therein lies a very large measure of its fascination.

If by either a combination of luck and skill; or if by the application of pure skill you do make the proper decision and do execute the correct course of action, and do shoot and scatter them, you are in business. That is if you are alone. If you have a hunting partner you can sit and wait for him to arrive. He will have started toward you at the sound of your shot, just as you would have started toward him at the sound of his.

If there are two of you, after he arrives you will jointly discuss how many there were, and which way they went, and whether or not you need to go and rescatter them, and do it—if you need to. Then you will sit and smoke, and talk about what good high school football players you both used to be, and how well you could hit inside curve balls, and how many girls used to chase each of you in such scandalous fashions, and how you won the war and other such lies—each of you generously accepting the other's statements at 20 percent above face value.

Sometimes if it is very cold you can build a very small fire and warm your frozen toes.

This is a lovely period. The work is done. Skill and intelligence have again triumphed and you need only sit down and philosophize expansively until the turkeys settle down. Then you may go and claim the just reward to which your expertise has so richly entitled you.

It is not until the turkeys have settled down that you can go off with any degree of assurance and begin to try to kill some. And often when you do start off, one turkey, who has been sitting in a tree within earshot the whole time, listening with interest to the entire discussion you have just completed, will take that opportunity to fly away.

Fall turkey hunting therefore falls into two broad categories, one of which is fairly hard and one of which is fairly easy. Leaving out luck, and leaving out the ones you stumble upon and kill, it is necessary to search for turkeys until you find them, and then take certain steps to get them scattered. This constitutes category one.

Category two is much simpler. In category two you hide and yelp and try to kill one. Many men who badmouth fall turkey hunting have either through luck or through the help of others stumbled into category two, and have never tried to do the first one, or have no real understanding of the difficulties involved there. Or in a lot of cases are simply too damned lazy to work their way through it.

If you are rich and powerful, or if you are laden with rank and position, you can get somebody to do category one for you. Sometimes your friends will do it for you, even though you are of modest rank and position, simply because they like you, although you will be expected to return the favor from time to time.

A man who calls you at night and tells you he has scattered a drove of turkeys in such and such a place, and either offers to take you with him in the morning, or send you there because he cannot go himself, has given you a gift that has involved a great deal of personal trouble.

I have done this—I have had it done for me. And I hope that when I get even older, and more withered, and feebler than I am now, that from time to time some younger and stronger and more vigorous man will draw upon his generosity and take pity on an old crock like me and do it again.

Category one calls for an immense amount of walking, mostly uphill, a high threshold of patience, and a pretty respectable amount of woodsmanship. It sometimes involves moving and working and not seeing anything all day. Many times you will have done all this all day long with no success, and then some thirty minutes before flying up time you will stop to listen. Since on still frosty evenings you can hear so far, you will sometimes hear turkeys flying up to roost a quarter of a mile away. Then you must start as quickly as you can toward them, and after you have gotten there and have gotten some of them to fly, and have shot in that direction to hasten the process, and have spent some few more minutes moving around to make sure you ran them all off, darkness falls.

Since you must be in the woods, hidden and ready at daybreak the next morning to join in the debating society when they begin to call one another back together, you are faced with the necessity of being able to find the same place again before daybreak. A place that you left after dark the evening before, that you saw when you were in a hurry and didn't pay a hell of a lot of attention to anyhow, and that you may now be approaching from the opposite direction.

This situation can cause some very interesting tours through the early morning darkness and can create some confusion even in the best of circles. Under such circumstances voices are seldom raised but eyebrows frequently are. The silence that falls when you have led two close personal friends three quarters of a mile to the wrong place one morning, and nobody hears a sound, is tomblike. You would rather they gathered around and stoned you than to be so damned forbearing and polite. You may take a degree of cold comfort in the knowledge that they too may have similarly sinned—but not that morning. That morning there are no sinners but you.

When you do get into the second category, where you hide and yelp and try to kill one, there is no question but that young turkeys will come to your calling more quickly in the fall than at any other time of the year. But at this season you have the added difficulty of identification.

Year-old gobblers are considerably bigger than year-old

hens, or even bigger than two-year-old hens for that matter. But they are not always going to be standing next to hens of either age so that you may have a chance to compare sizes. Neither are you going to be able to see a beard on year-old gobblers. The beard is there, but it is only an inch long and it is hidden under the feathers. You must, therefore, shoot year-old gobblers on the length of their legs or the coarseness of their voice, or their size, or the relative nakedness of their head. And as a consequence you are going to call up a hell of a lot of turkeys that you are going to look over as carefully as you can and then let walk off. If you saw young gobblers standing on golf courses, or in open pastures, or between year-old hens, your identification would be nearly a 100 percent. But in bad light, which is normal, or in patchy underbrush where you see only part of turkeys, or on flying turkeys, it is an awful lot easier to say than it is to do.

Old gobblers, on the other hand, are in my opinion a great deal more difficult to kill in the fall than they are in the spring. They will frequently go in little groups of three or four. They can be scattered, in fact sometimes they will flush wild a hundred and fifty yards ahead of you, but for some reason they seem to have much less flocking instinct than do younger birds. In some cases old turkeys seem perfectly willing to get back together next week, or the week after. Many times they are almost mute. They may come to your calling, but they will do it silently, and with painful slowness. Since you are restricted in your contact to the sound of their walking, if there is the least bit of wind you are not going to have any idea of where they are until they get there. I can recall a great many times when I gave such turkeys an hour or so to come back, became convinced that there was no turkey within a quarter of a mile of me, and when I got up to quit, ran one off.

This matter of wind needs a little more discussion.

In all your dealings with turkeys, the most valuable piece of equipment that you have is your ear, and the most used of your senses is your sense of sound. Your sense of hearing is so far superior to your sense of sight in this respect that I do really believe a blind man could kill more turkeys than a deaf man. You will hear infinitely more turkeys than you will ever see.

You will either hear them yelp, or you will hear them fly

when you flush them out of trees by accident, or you will hear them flying up to roost, or you will hear them scratching in the leaves. Occasionally you will hear them walking. In the spring you may hear them drum, or you will hear them gobble. The principal point I am trying to make is that the overwhelming amount of contact with turkeys is conducted through the sense of sound, and almost until the time you pull the trigger the entire affair is handled with the ears and not with the eyes.

Since contact therefore, is not only established but is maintained largely by sound, wind defeats you. It defeats you because it deafens you.

Wet leaves and wet woods are bad enough. Then you cannot hear anything walk, or scratch. You still have the sound of their wings if they fly, or the sound of their voices if they yelp or gobble, to establish contact. Wind, though, kills it all. Not only are whatever noises turkeys may make smothered under the rustling of leaves and branches, but the wind itself makes all sorts of strange sounds. A large part of the value of your sense of hearing is your sense of selective hearing. Squirrels sound like nothing else but squirrels. Deer walk in a completely distinctive fashion and unlike any other thing. The thrashers and the wrens and the warblers scratching in the leaves are perfectly recognizable as such.

The wind mixes all this up, adds some peculiar sounds of its own to the mixture and presents you with a potpourri of miscellaneous junk. Mysterious, miscellaneous junk. Sight and sight alone is simply not enough.

If turkeys were born without vocal chords, there would not be ten honestly called up and killed in this state every year. And if the wind blew all the time like it does in novels written by the Brontë sisters, then the annual ten would most likely drop to three.

I recognize that the wind usually blows in only one direction at a time. I recognize as well that not only is a turkey infinitely a man's superior in his ability to hear, but he is also as infinitely superior in his ability to assess what he does hear. He is far better able to sort out strange sounds from background noises. It would therefore logically follow that downwind turkeys could hear you call much farther than usual, and that even though you couldn't hear them answer, they would do so, and would come anyhow.

But as in so many other respects in regard to turkeys, logic does not necessarily buy the baby any shoes.

Logic leaves the baby barefooted in this particular instance because wind does something else to turkeys. It disrupts to a marked degree their marvelous ability to fix the direction of a sound—what in my end of the world is called "coursing" a sound. There is no way to adequately describe a turkey's ability to hear under any circumstances, but let me wander down this byway for a minute or two with an example.

Some years ago, back when I was in what was, to misquote the Bard, "my salad days, green of judgment, hot of blood," I hunted regularly in a county north of where I lived. It was in wonderful territory and I ought to have killed piles of turkeys. I didn't, I couldn't yelp, I couldn't cluck, I either moved too much or not enough. The only thing I didn't do wrong was to hunt out of season. But I had patience and I wanted turkeys.

One morning during the spring season, I was sitting on the forward slope of a long ridge, a hundred yards downhill from a woods road that ran along the top of the ridge at the edge of a pasture. I was well hidden—I did that even then—and from time to time I picked up my box yelper and made outrageous noises with it.

I didn't think then that the noises were outrageous. I considered them to be a perfect imitation of a turkey hen in the final stages of nymphomania.

Three turkeys, who were by no means coming to the racket I was making, but who were too young to be horrified by it, came down the hill fifty yards away and to my left. As they passed me they would from time to time stop and pick buds from sweetgum seedlings, or scratch through the leaves and pick up something from the ground.

One of these turkeys was somewhat bigger than the other two but although they were in plain sight I could see no beard. I was not sure then of the relative size differences between boys and girls and did not know about the difference in the length of the leg or the nakedness of a gobbler's head. I did, even then, know something about sex, and if somebody would have screwed somebody it would have given me a hint and I could have shot the one on top—turkeys are invariably conventional in such matters. But nobody did, and I had to let them all pass. When they were fully two hundred yards away all three of them stopped dead still, extended their necks to full length, and froze. They were alert, obviously preparing to run or fly and were clearly spooked. It must have taken two or three minutes before I heard what they had already heard at an additional range of two hundred yards, the sound of a car coming down the road in the edge of the pasture.

I have excellent ears, but they have never been in that class. Those turkeys heard the noise of that car, coursed it, identified it, and when it was passing behind me they had already relaxed and begun to feed again and move on. It was an humbling demonstration.

I hunt now as I hunted then, when I have the day off or can steal the day off. Whether it is raining or not, and whether it is windy or not, you are never going to kill any turkeys sitting around the house; so I go. Coincidence being what it is, some of the days I have had off or have stolen off, have been days with high wind. I have sometimes hunted on days when the wind was so high you felt obliged to hold onto trees to keep from being blown away. On some such days I have scattered turkeys or have found turkeys through luck, and have repeatedly seen turkeys approach my yelping from downwind. I have seen young turkeys walking at the right speed, and giving every other indication that they give when they are going to walk up into your lap, and I have seen them pass a hundred yards off the line, turning their heads from side to side trying to find me. These are only the ones I saw. Like all other contact with turkeys, you know that for every one that you do see there are dozens that you don't.

Wind is a lovely thing to sail boats with, and to run windmills. Poets must have it to move clouds and to dance daffodils. It is a fine thing for surfing and for moving ducks and for flying kites. It is a pain in the ass to try to hunt turkeys in.

Fall turkey hunting is a lot like saltwater fishing anyhow. You either stay out there all day and drown bait and drink beer, or you catch a boatful and after you get home you must spend half the night driving all around town trying to give away fish.

There are instances during the fall season when you get out

of the car and slam the door and scatter turkeys. When they settle down before you get your pipe lit. When they squall back every time you yelp, and when the young gobblers walk all over you in bunches and it is so easy you get ashamed of yourself.

And then there are those other days when you scatter a hell of a drove off the roost at dark. At daylight the next morning you get back to the same spot perfectly and sit down and it sounds as if you were sitting in the middle of a poultry farm. Turkeys are sailing through the woods like buzzards, trying to gather back together. There are gobbler fights in three directions. There is enough squalling and wing flapping and bedlam to make you think you were sitting in the middle of a drove of pterodactyls—assuming those things ran in droves.

In the middle of all this turmoil you will call up one four-pound hen who winks at you and walks off. When you finally realize they are almost back together and you get up to rescatter them they get away, and you end up standing there, inept, incompetent, frustrated and helpless, with a magnificent opportunity to be modest about your ability.

It would be the poorest possible time for a man to walk up to you and ask you for a raise. Category two ain't always easy.

If you are intelligent you are not ever going to talk about this kind of a day in front of non-turkey hunters. And the reason you had better not is that because to someone who never stood there, it is absolutely inconceivable that a man could be in the middle of that many turkeys and not kill one, unless he is lying about how many he saw. If you are dumb enough to talk about this at a cocktail party where alcohol has dulled both your native caution and everyone else's normal sense of politeness, you are going to get looks and expressions and comments that imply that you are not only of another species but perhaps are even a member of a separate genus. Especially if there is some clod present, and there always is, who has killed three turkeys in his life—two on deer stands and one while squirrel hunting, and you are going to have to stand there and listen to a solid thirty minutes of "there I was," stories.

The proper drill is one of careful reticence, and unless you have killed one, say in positive tones that you ain't seen a damned thing.

There is, you see, something about turkeys, unlike any other field of endeavor I am aware of, that creates instant experts.

One more aside.

Some years back, a good friend of mine stumbled over turkey hunting in between fishing trips and golf games and tried it a little. Somebody gave him a little cedar box and a piece of slate for a striker, and he sat around in his kitchen and learned to cluck. Nothing fancy, no subtleties, just a plain cluck.

He and I hunted together a good deal that year, and we hunted in some awfully good places. We both had friends who had turkeys and who were willing to let us chase them. Neither one of us had the faintest damned idea of what we were doing. We got too close and ran turkeys off. We stayed too far away so that turkeys couldn't hear us. We moved around too much and we did it too quickly. We didn't get picked up by the game warden and resist arrest, but as I recall it, that was about the only wrong we left righted. This friend, making every foolish error possible, and sunk in abysmal ignorance, went out and sat around in the woods and clucked every once in a while and killed three gobblers that spring—three gobblers any one of whom could have stood flat-footed and raped an ostrich. Every time you opened the county paper he seemed to be there again, standing in front of the newspaper office, smiling, and holding up an even bigger turkey. Unfortunately, he began to read his own press notices—he became an expert.

As people would begin to talk about old grizzled turkeys that had gobbled in the same hollow for the past three years and weighed at least twenty-five pounds, Harry would say, "Tell me where he is and I will go up there and kill him for you."

And the conversation would wither and die. Harry was a nice boy. He was likable and generous and personable, normally, but people began to dodge him and his advice, and they remembered—they usually do.

The next spring came; he and I went to the same places and did the same things, and the same sitting around on logs and stumps and clucking with the same box that had been so deadly the year before didn't work at all. The percentages began to even out. He started to get a little edgy.

Halfway through the season people were going out of their way to hunt him up and to call to him all the way across the courthouse square to ask him if he had killed anything yet. He began to walk around with his head down and big veins began to throb visibly in his temples when he talked about turkeys. He moved from edginess to frustration to frenzy, and the retrogression was rapid too.

By the last week of the season he was pitiful. He was spending thirty minutes at a time clucking at pileated woodpeckers. He was running across swamps a half mile wide to get to cawing crows. To my positive knowledge, because he did it in my direct sight, he spent the better part of two mornings slipping up on an old burn black stump in a straw field.

He never did kill one—he never even shot at one—he never even came close, and he closed the season a basket case. Becoming an unfrocked expert straightened him out, his natural sweetness of disposition re-surfaced, and he became again the pleasant, fumbling, ineffective and respectable turkey hunter we had all been used to. He is no longer the fountainhead of all skill and knowledge, and he kills one every once in a while now, too.

It goes the other way too sometimes, this disease of expertise.

Some seasons back an acquaintance of mine, a man who under normal circumstances killed a turkey every second or third year, killed four one spring. Two were run over him, one flew over him, and one he called up.

Never in all my life have I ever gotten so tired of hearing about anything or have begrudged a man his luck quite so bitterly. The man has become, and has remained, absolutely insufferable. He finds fault with your yelping and he disagrees with your tactics. Not even having been present at the engagement does not prevent him from telling you in detail and at length what you should have done and why. Even if you killed the turkey under discussion he will tell you how you could have done it quicker and more artistically.

He comments on your choice of hunting clothes, the gauge of your shotgun and your selection of shot sizes. He makes these statements and others, all unsolicited, in the kind of calm, reasonable and instructive tone of voice that puts your back up. He has appointed himself chairman of the board of wisdom.

Last spring he didn't kill one. Because I am by nature vengeful and vindictive, I was at first delighted. Then I realized that he had simply changed games.

He is now a teacher. He has become an instructor and a coach and an elder statesman and he will probably never kill one again. He will always manage to hunt in the company of someone whom he has under instruction and will, therefore, always have a built-in excuse. He was not trying to kill a turkey, he was just trying to call one up for Sam.

Like an old soldier who will never again be required to fight, he can be remarkably brave, for he will never be called upon to handle the dice again.

This is fall turkey hunting, split into two broad categories, one relatively hard, one sometimes easy, and sometimes impossible. It is often maligned, generally misunderstood and frequently overlooked. It is a pile of fun—but there is a better kind.

7

SPRING

Fall hunting is fun. It is as gay and bright and frothy as light summer literature. It smells good and it looks good and it feels good, but like making love to chorus girls, there ain't no depth to it.

Fall hunting is maneuvers.

Spring hunting is war.

In this latitude, thirty-one degrees north, as the equinox approaches and the earth begins to tilt, increasing day length triggers sexual activity in turkeys. Light indirectly activates the reproductive organs in both male and female by first stimulating the pituitary through the nervous system. The initial stimulus is received through the skin as well as through the eyes.

Yearling gobblers, who by now weigh twelve pounds, are of course affected along with other turkeys. But in this, their first spring, they gobble little if at all. Substantial evidence exists to the effect that they are not yet sexually mature and that they are incapable of fertilizing eggs.

The overwinter droves break up and the hens begin to go off singly or in small groups. The yearling gobblers break off into little droves by themselves, and they hush.

This group of yearling gobblers, the same turkeys who two months ago were vocal to the point of rudeness, become the most reticent. They creep about like wraiths and like well-behaved small boys are seen but seldom heard.

Gobblers who are in their second year or older begin to

seek out and establish gobbling grounds, areas technically known as leks. And these turkeys, who two months previously were almost sphinxlike in their silence, become the most vocal of all.

They are vocal for exactly one reason. They are thinking of girls.

Turkey hens lay fertile eggs for a period of up to a month after mating because crypts in the wall of the upper oviduct serve as sperm reservoirs. Movement of the sperm from the infundibulum crypts to the lumen of the duct is largely mechanical. Ovum enters the Fallopian funnel, passes through the infundibulum magnum, distends the infundibulum, and the sperm are squeezed into contact with the passing ovum.

All of this is technically correct, all of it is scientifically accurate and not a word of it need concern any of us.

What concerns us here is not science, nor medical polysyllables, but the other part, the good part, the part the young turkeys talk about when they hang around the poolroom. The part where the sperm is introduced into the oviduct.

It is upon the introduction of that sperm that you must base both your strategy and your tactics, because the behavior of a turkey gobbler at this season of the year is wholly keyed to such an introduction.

A turkey gobbler cannot read or write. He neither speaks nor understands Latin, and he would not know an infundibulum crypt if he met one in the road.

But in matters concerning the introduction of the sperm into the oviduct he is a goddamn jewel.

From the middle of May until the first of the following March a turkey gobbler is straightforward. He is reliable, he is sober and sedate and reasonable. There may from time to time pass through his head erotic flashes of pleasant passages last spring, but these constitute no more than twinkles in his eye.

Upon occasion, possibly in an excess of fond recollection, he may gobble once or twice. Perhaps this is simply to clear his throat, or perhaps it is just for old times sake. But principally throughout this period of his year he conducts himself and his business with the disciplined dignity of retired Colonels in their seventies.

Retired Colonels of artillery, with white moustaches.

78

Upon your first meeting with him you would unhesitantly cash his check, solicit his advice on municipal bonds, or approach him hat in hand for a donation to build the county orphanage. He looks and acts as if he were about to be elected Chairman of the Board of Censors.

And then spring comes, and on or about the first of March his behavior patterns change, and the transition of Dr. Jekyll into Mr. Hyde is by comparison a minor aberration.

Dignity not only drops from his shoulders, he uses it to wipe his feet.

The wattles at the base of his neck swell and grow red. Instead of standing still he shifts his weight from one foot to the other all the time, as if the ground were hot. The set of his head upon his neck is different—it leans forward, looking for something. If he had eyebrows, one eyebrow would be raised all the time.

His feathers brighten and take on an iridescence they have not shown previously. He approaches the world and everything in it with the thought processes of a twenty-year-old who has been at sea for eighteen months.

There is in the air around him an electricity, a magnetism, an aura of bright danger—he is cocked.

He is single-minded, dedicated and sole-purposed. There is nothing on his mind but girls.

Girls for breakfast, girls for lunch, girls in the middle of the afternoon. Girls for tea and girls for dinner and girls before he goes to bed. And when he does go to bed he flies up and cranes his neck in all directions to pick out the roosting places of nearby girls in order that he will not take a single step in the wrong direction when getting an early start on tomorrow's girls.

None of this interferes with his native caution or with his ingrained suspicion in any way, rather one set of emotions is overlain upon the other; or one instinct upon the other, if you prefer.

The two emotions experienced concurrently make him almost vibrate. I suspect that close to, he hums, like high-voltage lines.

His sole purpose in life is lovemaking—as often as possible, as rapidly as possible, and with as many partners as possible.

He begrudges the night when he must sleep and thereby interrupt the pressing business of his days.

He is cocked—all the time.

So single-functioned and so dedicated is he in his purpose now, that he frequently neglects to eat. A gobbler who means it and is tending to his business (and during this time of the year it is difficult to find a gobbler who is not so occupied) will quite often lose two or three pounds during the spring—an amount that approaches 20 percent of his body weight.

He will strut and drum for as much as half an hour at a time. Strutting is technically supposed to be done to attract the female, and to do it he drops his wings until their ends drag upon the ground. I have seen turkeys who had worn off the outer four or five primaries, strutting, as cleanly as if they had been cut off with scissors. When he struts he stands the tail feathers upright and spreads them out in a fan. His head is drawn back in between what would be his shoulders, if he had shoulders, and he walks in a measured and stately manner.

I am not a hen turkey, and therefore presumably cannot adequately judge what is attractive to a hen turkey, but my private opinion is that he looks ridiculous.

A creature who is normally the epitome of slim, sleek alertness, whose feathers lie close to the body, smooth and luminous to the point of being burnished, who normally moves as if all his joints were oiled, turns all of a sudden into a clumsy ball. Every feather looks as if it had been plucked out and then glued back on, wrong side to. The neck, which had a sinuous, flowing and nearly serpentine grace is cramped back into his shoulders in the posture of a retired eighty-year-old bookkeeper with arthritis.

But there is no accounting for tastes, and he is not attempting to attract aging ex–timber markers but girl turkeys.

He drums often. This sound, which Audubon calls the pulmonic puff, defies description. It is not, to me at any rate, audible at distances beyond seventy or eighty yards. A poor approximation of its sound is to say "shut" as quickly and as explosively as you can with the tongue against the front teeth, and then say "varoom" in two syllables, with the "oom" coming up out of the diaphragm and drawn out and resonated against the roof of the mouth as much as possible. When I hear it in the woods I do not so much hear the sound as I feel it under my breast bone. It is ventriloquistic, pervading and is a sensation partway between sound and vibration.

This sound is far from ridiculous. It personifies wildness and solitude and lonely places. Nothing in my experience approaches it in this respect except the wild, far off calling of geese at night, drifting down out of an early autumn sky.

A turkey even during this season does naturally have to eat a little. He is after all a bird, and the metabolic processes of a bird are far more active than those of any mammal, saving some of the shrews. There are birds for instance with body temperatures of 105°F when normal, and with extremely fast heartbeats. And while a turkey is not keyed to the same pitch as a warbler, he is tuned pretty high. But during this period he eats seldom and what he does eat he eats quickly, and acts as if everything he took was tasteless. He is edgy and fidgety and nervous and appears to have his nerve ends not only exposed, but sticking out an inch or two, like antennae.

He has become not so much a bird as a psychological force. He reminds you of a good general. When you are in the company of the right kind of general officer you are not so much in contact with a man as you are with a presence. A turkey, tuned to the pitch at which he stays throughout the spring, is such a presence.

There is a term used in falconry that covers the situation.

When a falcon is at the peak of his training—when he is at the very top of his physical condition, humming with electricity and latent fierceness, he is said to be in Yarak. A turkey at this season of the year is likewise in Yarak.

It is at this point in time that the season opens, and it is in this month that you are allowed to seek him out on his own ground and try to kill him.

And it is principally because of what he is now that it is so shameful to ambush him at long range with a rifle or to murder him from a vehicle. To do so degrades you both.

He will now stake out his own territory, his lek, and restrict his movements largely to that location. He may move away some from time to time, go off to visit maybe, but it is not at all uncommon to find the same turkey gobbling on the same five acres every morning and roosting there at night, too.

81

He will gobble a little in the afternoon. He often gobbles once after he flies up to roost at night, but he gobbles primarily first thing in the morning. And he will begin to gobble sometimes as much as fifteen or twenty minutes before daylight, especially if he is a river swamp turkey.

River swamp turkeys for some reason begin to gobble noticeably earlier on any given morning than do hill turkeys. And from the standpoint of the hunter it is fortunate that they do so. As clean and open as a big river swamp can be, you would never be able to get close enough to call him if he waited till daylight to begin. He would see you coming and hush, a long time before you got there, if you couldn't go to him in the dark.

On any morning that you go to hunt you will be in the woods at daylight or preferably fifteen minutes before. You will have left your car and will have walked to the place from which you intend to listen. And then you are going to prop your gun up against a tree and wait.

If you have gotten there as early as you should, the first thing you are going to hear is nothing. Nothing but you is up yet. The only birds awake are a few owls and an occasional tardy whip-poor-will that hasn't knocked off and gone home to bed. Deer are still abroad, and you will hear them shuffling off ahead of you or boiling in herds out of thickets with all the ill-bred snorting and blowing of which they are capable. Possums and coons will still be prowling and you will hear some of these. But all of these things are night creatures that are supposed to be up. The only day creature there is you.

Just as the sky in the east begins to change from black into a steely blue-white, the owls will begin to sound off, and then the cardinals, and late in the spring, the yellow-billed cuckoos. These three birds make by far the most noise, though there are dozens and dozens of lesser bird noises in the background.

I have no idea how far you can hear an owl—one who is really leaning into his hoot and means it. I sometimes think it is like the folk song, the one that says "you can hear the whistle blow a hundred miles," but it is a hell of a long way, and early in the morning like this, most of them sound as if they were calling from across the River Styx.

It is a lovely time of the year. There is as yet not much color to the woods but there are some early hints and stirrings, mostly muted pastels or pale chalks with only two or three brights for contrast. The shrub form of buckeye is in full leaf and flower, and the red maple is in fruit. Both the buckeye flower and the maple seed are a bright red—a gaudy, primitive, barbaric red. Blackberry, sweetgum, and huckleberry will be in the beginning of early leaf in the understory, and witch hazel, tag alder and river birch in the middle story with both stories in pale, pale greens. All the oaks are in catkins, the long fuzzy strings that come before the leaf, and make a background of pale buff and brown. Dogwood shows occasional streaks of sharp white, and in the river swamps the yellow top makes splashes of chromium yellow.

Only rarely, and then only early in the year is there a hint of frost. Mostly the forest floor is a flat brown. Other than the floor, none of the colors are in masses but the catkins of the oaks. The sharper colors occur as isolated highlights scattered here and there at random.

When the owls come into full voice, just at daylight, turkeys will often gobble back at them. I don't know why turkeys gobble at owls but they do, and most men who kill a lot of turkeys have learned to do at least a presentable imitation of an owl, and do it.

Turkeys gobble primarily for girls, either to attract them or to let other turkey gobblers know they are on the job; that the situation is comfortably in hand, and that they need no help in handling anything that comes up. They can handle all the girls in hearing, thank you. But they do have a proclivity for gobbling at sudden sounds. Sometimes I think they may do it for the same reason that a man shouts in the woods. For high spirits, just for the hell of it, to hear it ring down through the trees and hear the echo come back.

Turkeys will, for I have heard them, gobble at sawmill whistles, at train and tugboat horns, at thunder, at owls as we said, at the slamming of a car door, at crows and at each other. Once, on an artillery range, I heard two turkeys gobble at the sound of the first round arriving at the registration point.

The purpose in hooting like an owl (I do not really recommend slamming car doors or firing off artillery pieces) is to get a turkey to gobble who didn't really mean to do it—finesse him into it as it were.

There are mornings when every turkey in the county will begin to gobble at daylight, and will do it so much it sounds as if he were in danger of choking himself. The very next morning you can go and stand in yesterday's footprints, as far as you can tell under identical conditions of wind, temperature and barometric pressure, and you will stand in the midst of silence.

These are the days when you must trick him into gobbling, or surprise him into it, because until he gobbles you do not know where he is and so you cannot get to him. You want to get within two hundred yards of the tree he is sitting in, gobbling, before he flies down, in order to try to call him to you from there. You want, very badly, to get there before he flies down if you can, and you have absolutely no idea of how long that is going to be. Sometimes he will stay on the limb fifteen minutes, sometimes an hour and a half, and since you never know ahead of time which one it will be you need to get there quickly. Since it is possible for you to hear him at half a mile or better, it makes for an awfully interesting athletic contest conducted at daylight in the woods on calm spring mornings. The fat businessman's quarter-mile dash, with shotgun.

The reason you want to get to him so quickly is that unlike with men, courting with turkeys goes both ways, girls seeking out boys if anything even more avidly than the reverse, and your chances are immensely improved if you can get to his tree before the ladies do. They can come in from the opposite direction of course and shut you off, but if you are quick you will be right half the time at least. Furthermore, so long as he stays in the tree and gobbles, you know exactly where he is. After he flies down he is apt to move. You can tell if he is still up, or if he has flown down by the sound of his gobble; it sounds considerably muffled and has less clarity after he is on the ground.

The point is though, that until he gobbles the first time, either on his own or until you have tricked him into it, you could be within a hundred yards of a turkey in the dark, or be beyond three quarters of a mile from one and not know the difference.

We ought to talk about this business of getting too close a little more.

In order to kill turkeys you have to go into the woods where they live. When you go into the woods you have the possibility of running turkeys off, if there were any living there to begin with. You cannot help this, no matter how stupid it makes you feel, you have to go in there. Some people though, have a great deal more talent for running turkeys off the roost than do other people.

Until now I have made an honest effort to keep self-aggrandizement out of these discussions.

I cannot hold it back any longer.

When a man does something superlatively well, it becomes false modesty not to admit it. Nobody likes a braggart; and false modesty may be the most obnoxious form of bragging known to man.

There is one thing that I do better than any man alive, or maybe better than any man who ever lived, and the time to talk about it is now.

For better than twenty years now, during the spring season, I get up early, I have a light breakfast, generally coffee and a sweet roll that I have in the car on the way to the woods—mostly I hunt alone. About the time I get to the woods, and have walked to the place from which I intend to listen and have propped my gun up against a tree and lit my pipe, my time comes. I formed the habit some years ago of taking along a wad of toilet paper against this time—dry leaves crumple so, and the green ones you pull up in the dark are sometimes poison oak which turns out later on to have been unwise.

I have learned that it is going to happen at this time of the morning, the hot coffee and the mild exercise and the time of day and so forth—it always does.

I do hereby state without equivocation that I have run more turkeys off the roost by moving my bowels under the tree in which they roosted than any man alive. I am the world's champion. There is not even a second place—I doubt that there is even anybody a close third.

If a man had formed the habit of standing next to me every day on spring mornings while I took my pants down at daylight, with his gun held at high port and with the safety off, that man, if he were a good shot, would have killed so many turkeys he would have become a public scandal. Fish and game departments would have his picture tacked up on the wall of post offices along with the F.B.I.'s list of the ten most wanted men.

85

This has happened to me so much that it is eerie. There has got to be voodoo involved, and the second sight, and visions. It has happened to me so much that I have come to expect it to happen now and feel a peculiar sense of loss when it does not.

I do not know when the last turkey was seen in Central Park. Undoubtedly before the park was so named and designated, and probably around 1720 or so, but it does not matter. If the New York City chapter of the Audubon Society wants to add the sighting of a wild turkey to the life list of those of its members who do not have it, I am available. If the New York Police Department will permit it, they need only invite me up next April. Call an early morning meeting and let me take my shotgun and my toilet paper and go into Central Park at daylight. If the ladies will promise to avert their eyes (I have an old-fashioned modesty in these matters) I will go to the nearest oak tree, take my pants down, and guarantee them the sight of a turkey flying out of that tree. East or west, whichever way he flies there is ample lighting on either Park Avenue or Broadway for them to be able to see him clearly outlined against the buildings.

The Lord imparts the strangest skills to some of His creatures.

Everybody, you know, ought to be able to do one thing really well, and most men can. Some men are at their finest when charging into machine gun nests in a blind rage. Some men can hit .428 on curve balls at the knees. There are men who paint, there are men who sculpt, there are men who are magnificent with the second barrel on charging tigers. The principal disadvantage these gentlemen all have is that they often show a tendency to exhibit their work or to discuss their feats to the utter boredom of their acquaintances or of the general public. The advantage that the public has with me and my skill, modest though it may be, is that unlike some of the owners of these more spectacular skills, I never discuss mine. Not that I haven't tried, but it somehow never seems to come up. It is a trifle difficult to casually work it into the normal everyday conversation.

Ah well, Gray says it beautifully:

"Full many a flower is born to blush unseen and waste its sweetness on the desert air."

Presumably my reward will come in a later life.

A turkey can gobble only one time and give you direction. But direction is only half of what you need. The other necessary element you need is distance, and unless he is very close when he first gobbles, you cannot tell exactly how far away he is. Experience will help you here to a degree, but a turkey can gobble at different levels of volume. If he is still on the roost when he gobbles he could be facing toward you, which makes it sound one way, or he could be looking in the other direction, which changes the level of the sound and helps to build confusion.

It is generally considered safest to start toward him the minute you hear him, and if he will gobble three or four more times at reasonably spaced intervals, you can get his location fixed and get to the proper place to try to kill him.

All kinds of things can happen during this procedure, which in military circles is called a movement to contact.

Assuming he did not sound so far away when he first gobbled that you considered it impossible, you can, because you know the country, know that there is impassable water between you and him and so you cannot go. Or you can start and find some obstacle in your way that you were not aware of. Later in the spring, with many of the trees in leaf and the woods thickening, sound carries much more poorly. A turkey that sounds as loud the last of April as he sounded the last of March may be three hundred yards nearer than he sounds. It adds one more little uncertainty to what is often already a cloudy affair.

You can start toward a gobbling turkey who is so far away that he does not gobble regularly enough for you to get there. This can be the most frustrating of all. You go as far as you dare, and then stand there shifting from one foot to the other. You don't know whether to sit where you are and yelp at imagination, or to keep going in what you think is the proper direction at the very real risk of running him off or hushing him up.

The point to be taken here, though, is that whether he gobbled on his own, or whether you have tricked him into doing it, he almost has to do it more than once unless he is very close, and throughout the whole approach the contact having been established by him must be maintained by him. During this period you are absolutely under his control and are utterly at his whim.

There are some very old and very wise turkeys who gobble

only a little bit. They cannot be tricked into gobbling very much and they are often silent for two or three days consecutively. If you can find the area one of them is using, you can then go back day after day because even if he is silent, the contact has been partially established—but only partially. Four or five acres is a big place, even if he roosts on the same four or five acres nightly, and he can just as easily be on one side of it as he can be on the other. In such a situation he can perhaps be best located the night before. On still afternoons the sound he will make flying up to roost is so loud as to be shocking after sitting in the quiet for so long. But you must then sit there until darkness comes and lets you slip out, if he is close, and then come back at daylight in the morning.

These kind are tough. These are the kind that people spend the season with. These are the kind that if you do finally kill, you stand and look down upon with real regret because you have established such a close rapport over the days or weeks it took you to kill him.

I have never picked up one like this after killing him without a real sense of loss, a little bit sorry that I had done it, but not sorry enough to quit.

Again, while I have no log book to refer to, nor any documents to consult, in thinking back over the years I feel that in dealing with gobbling turkeys you will kill one for every three or four that you work.

Some turkeys are just not going to come. No skill, no expertise in yelping, no combination of moves and countermoves is going to make the least particular of difference. There is no egotism in this either. I do not intend to imply that if I cannot kill a certain turkey then nobody else can kill him either, or that what is impossible for me, is impossible for anyone. I have been humbled and humiliated far too many times to have any shred of an illusion left. I have given turkeys away to experts. To men I knew were experts, who tried three or four or five times and then offered them back. But I had already abandoned hope, and left it abandoned.

There just happen to be turkeys that will gobble on the roost a hundred times. Turkeys you can get to quickly, and hide from easily, and do everything perfectly, and be at the right place at the right time. Turkeys who will then fly down and gobble three hundred times on the ground over a period of two hours. Turkeys who will then come to within eighty yards of where you sit and not one step further. Turkeys who will parade and strut and drum there, and who wild horses could not drag that last twenty steps.

And there are a thousand stories about what you ought to do to kill them.

I have listened to men seriously discuss scratching in the leaves behind them with their hands, to imitate turkeys feeding. I have heard men say with a perfectly straight face that they took off their hat and slapped it repeatedly on their leg to imitate the wing flapping of a gobbler fight. You can get sacks full of advice about gobbling back at turkeys, or drumming back at them. I have heard all my life nearly, that if a turkey ever answers you he will come there eventually even if you have to sit until noon to wait for him. Maybe he will, but if it takes him that long the hell with it. I am not about to sit in the woods till noon listening to squirrels and bluejays while waiting for turkeys that may be a mile and a half off.

I have never tried scratching in the leaves either, or hitting my leg with my hat. I have never done so because I am convinced that it is going to sound exactly like a man scratching in the leaves with his hand or hitting his leg with his hat.

Gobbling back, I am willing to admit, may work, may be even rarely worth trying. Drumming is just barely within the realm of possibility. But I regard the large body of all this kind of advice as being in the same category as saying, "Kitty, kitty, kitty," or standing up and whistling and calling "Here, Rattler, here."

I am a big believer in moving. I think that unless a gobbler comes in very quickly, one of the most difficult things in the world is to firmly plant your ass under a tree and stubbornly refuse to move an inch until you have called the turkey up and killed him.

A great many turkeys will come to your calling from the roost and will then take up a regular pattern of movement, first toward you and then away. Never coming close enough to shoot and never getting out of hearing, and all the time gobbling every thirty seconds or so. You know where they are every minute of the time but a fat lot of good it does you. I have upon occasion waited them out to the other end of their track, yelped once to turn them back, and then gotten up and ran a fast forty yards toward them and hidden quickly and shut up. Occasionally they will come back gobbling, and when they do stop they are forty yards closer than they think they are, and you can point out this error to them with a Battery, one round.

On just as many occasions I have jumped up to perform this ingenious maneuver and when I got forward and hid I did not ever hear another sound. This led me to believe that the turkey was not as far away as I thought he was when I moved, and when he saw me move he ran off. I have gotten up to move, either forward, or to get around turkeys, and have heard them go off on the ground gobbling until they faded out of hearing.

One example will serve.

Some three or four years ago I was in the process of leaving the woods one spring morning, having heard nothing. On the way back to the car I stopped and yelped down a small hollow that ran northeasterly away from the back end of some abandoned fields down toward the backwater.

A turkey gobbled back instantly, no more than two hundred yards away. I stepped just out of the edge of the fields, cut three or four huckleberry bushes to stick for a blind, sat down with my back against a big pine, stuck my bushes, and waited. Immediately to my front and running downhill from left to right was a gentle hollow, thickly stocked with young sweetgum eight or ten inches in diameter. The floor of this hollow, except for an occasional downed log, was as clean as a park.

Across the hollow and also running right down to the edge of the backwater was what is called a two-aged stand of pine. Loblolly and shortleaf of large diameter, but short, limby as hell, and with a bole taper like inverted ice cream cones. Under this overstory was a fairly well-stocked stand of pine seedlings, six inches high and up, but clean enough to see through well. The far side of the gum hollow, where it bordered the pine, was about eighty yards away.

It was after seven-thirty in the morning, far too late for a turkey to be gobbling that much unless he were alone, and a bright sunny day without a breath of wind.

Turkeys who gobble very much at this late hour generally

have not yet gathered up a harem. And if two and a half hours of daylight have gone by without a girl, they tend to consider themselves to be two and a half hours in arrears and are rather desperately anxious to correct what has become a disgraceful situation.

This turkey was alone—because I saw him.

He would approach, gobbling, walk south toward me along the backwater, come to the far side of the gum hollow, stop, drum, strut and pirouette, walk back and forth, turn around and go back north, still gobbling. He would go out of sight among the pine seedlings, keep going until by the sound of him I would judge him to be two hundred yards away, and when at this point I would yelp, he would turn around and come back and do the same thing all over again.

Gobbling every minute, he did this four or five times.

Finally, I waited him out to the far side of his range, put all the sex I could scrape up into one yelp, jumped up and ran down to the bottom of the gum hollow and lay flat behind a log. This time when he came back, he stopped eighty yards from where I lay.

Next, I let him get back to the far side of his range again, got up and ran back past my original blind by the pine tree, went fifty yards out into the fields, yelped like Cynthia calling to Propertius, and then did the hundred in a flat twelve seconds to get back to my log in the bottom of the gum hollow. I beat him back alright, and he came back alright, but he came back and stopped within a goddamn inch of where he had stopped the first time.

Cursing all turkeys, I let him get all the way out again, yelped, and got up and made a long fast circle back out through the fields, northwest through some mixed pine and hardwood thickets, and then due east down to the edge of the backwater to a point I judged was within gunshot of the northernmost end of his range. I couldn't yelp when I first got there, having to devote all my attention to breathing.

He raised all sorts of hell down where I had just come from and when I finally gathered up enough air to yelp, he answered at once and started up toward me. So help me God, he stopped ten yards out of gunshot and went through the same business of strutting and drumming and fanning his tail and walking off.

I stayed up there and got humiliated again a time or two and then yelped again, got up again, went halfway back around him and got down to within range of the backwater and midway along his track. He was passing by when I started down the hill toward him so I had to wait to let him go by before moving down to wait for him to come back.

I sat there, listening to him gobble, knowing he had to come right back by me, and drowning in self-esteem. I felt exactly like the man in Twain's line, the man "With the calm confidence of a Christian, with four aces."

He stayed up on the north end, where I had just come from, as firmly as if he had been tied to a tree and gobbled until I got tired of hearing him.

At eleven-thirty I got up and walked up there and ran the bastard off, yelling "shoo" as loud as I could.

He flew out over the backwater looking roughly the size of a moa. Turkeys that big really ought to be shot with double-barreled lion rifles. They might charge if they were only wounded and you could get yourself in a hell of a shape if you did not have positive stopping power in the second barrel.

Just because moving works once does not make it a sovereign remedy, and turkeys, no matter what turkey hunters may feel about it, don't have to do anything.

One final word on the whole subject. As much as I believe in it personally and feel comfortable doing it, and recommend it every chance I get, there are places and instances where moving is impossible.

A big river swamp is one of those places.

In the first place it is absolutely flat in there. There may be six-inch ridges from time to time and there are eight-inch depressions, where overcup oak grows. There are some striking falls of a foot and a half down into tupelo or cypress ponds, but there is no other relief—none. In the fall when the sloughs dry up you can get down into the bottom of the slough bed, some six or eight feet below the normal floor, but only for this particular period of the year. Taking advantage of the terrain to move about in river swamps must be left out of your bag of tricks. In almost every case there, you can sit down and see a man walking a quarter of a mile away.

Except in exceptional instances, attempting to move on turkeys in this area is stupid. There will be all kinds of situations that arise with turkeys two hundred yards off and in absolutely plain sight and no matter how badly you want to do it, you cannot move.

If there is a rule for river swamps it may be stated simply that where you sit is where you stay.

In plain fact the mere selection of a place to hide and call from in there is extremely difficult. There are some blowdowns, of course, and some places where tangles of vines wrap around the bases of trees. After the timber has been cut, if single tree selection or patch clear cutting were used, there will be clumps of briars and some low seedlings. Yellow top in the spring will make thick clumps of foliage, often too thick, and there are some patches of palmetto. By and large, though, if you hunt in river swamps, whatever you intend to hide behind you must bring into the swamp with you. Whether you use a roll of camouflage netting or intend to cut bushes, you had better have them with you when you go. In there, as in *Macbeth*, Birnam Wood must come to Dunsinane.

And you have to hide. Hill or swamp, in the spring you have got to do it. There is all sorts of evidence to suggest that a turkey is color blind. Maybe he is. But he can damn well tell dark colors from light ones, and he is the world's best at picking out motion. Picking it out at a long distance too.

Perhaps in the early fall, if a man could sit with the utter stillness of a professional naturalist he could depend upon calling up young gobblers, remaining immobile against a dark background, and raising the gun to shoot in one motion at the last. I say maybe only because I am willing to listen to another man's point of view, not because I really believe in it.

To go through life in the spring, dealing with old gobblers, attempting to sit out in the open and depending upon immobility to get the job done, is folly.

Nobody, nowhere, no time, is going to get away with it on anything like a regular basis.

8

TECHNIQUES

The very last intention I have, or ever had, was to sit down here and construct a "how to do it manual." You have no doubt seen a hundred and I have seen a thousand.

"There I was, and there he was, and I killed him dead at forty yards." They weary you with the titles before you ever get to the instruction.

But if you shoot turkeys you are going to have to shoot them with something, and the state of Alabama has been remarkably generous in not promulgating edicts concerning what you may or may not shoot them with.

There have been, from time to time, mutterings by people like me trying to get the state to outlaw rifles. There is little hope for it, though, because any state that will cold-bloodedly let people run deer with dogs is not apt to concern itself with something like a rifle-shot turkey. I am not mad at the state about this, simply disappointed; it is just one of the trials of life, like a wife coming in with fourteen pairs of shoes. You won't get a divorce because of it, just cry a little.

You may shoot turkeys with anything you wish.

We even have a bow hunting season in Alabama. It starts some two weeks before the regular season in the fall and I believe these gentlemen may get an extra week or so in the spring though I don't keep up with it. So far, I have not heard of a turkey being killed with a bow.

I am aware that the weapon has ample power to do it with.

In addition to bows winning the battle of Agincourt, I seem to remember reading that an elephant or two has been killed with one.

The difficulty lies not in the power, or lack of it, but in the motion and in the ground cover. Small twigs and branches will deflect arrows I am told, and it is rather common to have to shoot turkeys through holes the size of your hand. Some of the bows I see advertised in the sporting goods catalogues have pulling weights of forty to sixty pounds, and there have to be very few men who can present this weapon, drawn, and hold the draw for half an hour, as it is normal to have your shotgun across one knee with your face down on the stock for half an hour.

I cannot imagine any old turkey that came up on the ground standing there in absorbed interest while a man lifted his bow and drew the arrow to his cheek. I think bow hunters must have to take an awful lot of shots at the tail end of turkeys who are stretched out in a full run.

Somebody is surely going to kill one eventually. Someone probably already has, and may write me a letter and in tones of outraged innocence point out that he was killing turkeys with a bow before I was born, and by the way, what the hell do I think the Indians did anyhow?

I hope someone does. I will read it with interest but with no faintest thoughts of imitation. For one thing the Indians had a few more turkeys to work with than we do, and for another, I have sufficient difficulty with a shotgun to keep me occupied all the rest of the way to the boneyard. Any man who has called up turkeys and killed them with a bow is entitled to wear a sign all the rest of his life, a sign which has printed on it in large letters, "I am a better man than you are." I will cheerfully step off the sidewalk and take my hat off to let him pass in complete agreement.

But as I say, you can shoot almost anything because the whole area operates in a fine spirit of dealer's choice. If you are deadly with a Model 1911, Colt .45 caliber pistol you can use that, and call them up and shoot their heads off. You can even stand up and invite them to get away before you draw, if you like it that way.

You can lie around on the edges of pastures with a 3500-

foot-per-second rifle and turn twenty-pound gobblers into feathers and turkey soup, if that is your choice.

If you are man enough to carry it, you can buy a double-barrelled magnum ten gauge and send a quarter of a pound of shot down through the woods every time you pull the trigger.

My state does not even require a plug in semi-automatic weapons on resident game; so you can get a three-inch magnum twelve gauge and fill it up with five, 4½ drachm shells.

If you are particularly deadly, and have an icy temperament and a rocklike hand, you can call them up and shoot them very carefully in the head with a Colt Woodsman using .22 shorts.

I can't do any of these things. I shoot a Colt .45 well enough to kill people but not well enough to kill turkeys. I ain't big enough to carry a ten gauge magnum much farther than the front yard, and my native good taste won't let me lie around the edges of pastures and ambush two hundred yard turkeys with a minute of angle rifle. So I do it with a plain twelve gauge shotgun and one of the standard loads.

We have some highly opinionated schools around here on shot sizes and some very pronounced opinions on what size a man ought to use. There are a great many men who use only size 7½ shot, bought in what are called high-velocity loads. Their thesis holds that it is absolutely outrageous to shoot turkeys anywhere but in the head, and that the small shot gives such dense patterns out there, that nothing else should ever be used.

There is a big shot school, who, largely influenced by goose hunters, uses nothing smaller than magnum 2s and shoot at the whole turkey. I shot magnum 2s for several years and did some outstanding things with them. I remember killing a flying gobbler scattered off the roost late one afternoon with one pellet. It went up through the breast, breaking the sheet of bone that separates the two sides of the breast throughout its length, entered the vitals and killed the turkey. There was not another shot mark in him. I shot him when he was directly overhead, and he stopped his forward motion and stayed there; flying hard but neither gaining nor losing altitude nor making any forward progress either. I stood under him for a long time—it is not usual to see a turkey imitating a hovering helicopter—prepared to shoot again. It was not necessary. He began to lose height slowly, and still flying, settled down in front of me and expired.

I told this story to the point of nauseous boredom, bought a presentation box of magnum 2s, and went all over the country on missionary trips singing the praises of this load and forcing two or three shells on friends and acquaintances and even on total strangers and urging them to switch over. There are people who have not spoken to me since.

I next missed several turkeys at fifty yards, who were behind trees with only their head and neck exposed; became disenchanted and changed schools, and went to the other extreme.

I can remember quoting excerpts from ballistic manuals to the effect that the shocking power of a load was proportional to the square of the number of pellets striking, regardless of the weight of the individual pellet, and that you really ought to shoot turkeys with 9s, but since you couldn't buy high base 9s you had to drop back to 7½s.

Some of the same people I hunted up to press 7½s upon I had been to three years before to proselytize into using magnum 2s. It led to a lack of confidence in the prophet. He had changed religions too many times.

I have finally settled on 4s but I don't try to convince anybody else to use them.

Fine shot is great if you only shoot turkeys on the ground, inside forty yards, and invariably in the head. But if you only knock him down, and he is struggling and flopping off, or if you miss him wholly, and he is flying off, you are going to feel a strong sense of inadequacy standing there shooting an eighteen-pound bird in the ass at fifty yards with 7½s.

Fours seem to me to give presentable patterns at forty yards, where like everybody else, I shoot only at heads. But for the second shot, or the third, or when they are flying back over my head, I shoot at turkeys—all of turkeys.

My sainted grandfather used to say that the head of a turkey is the same size as the body of a dove. He said that if you can hit a dove you ought to be able to hit the head of a flying turkey as well. This is an accurate statement and his assessment of the relative sizes of the two objects is correct. But he was a man who normally shot four cases of shells a year and who disdained to shoot at any ducks but pintails and canvasbacks. A man who was perfectly capable of putting the edge of the pattern on close in ducks, so as not to overkill them and spoil the meat. Since he is no longer around to supervise my education, I intend to keep on disgracing him and shooting flying turkeys in the all over. And casual, slapdash, careless, whippersnappers like me feel a lot more comfortable with bigger shot while we commit this dastardly act.

I have some friends who start with a 7½ in the chamber, followed by a 4 in the magazine, backed up by a 2. This is a solution, unless you have to take the first shot at a flying turkey. It also involves all kinds of business with the flashlight before you leave the car, fumbling in various pockets and trying to read shot sizes printed on the sides of plastic shells you have carried for three weeks and the printed numbers of which have consequently become unreadable.

It is all a matter of personal preference anyhow. Whatever you feel you can do it with, you ought to use. I decline to be inveigled into any more arguments about it. If a man asks me what shot size I use, I tell him. If he asks me why, I have formed the habit of telling him that I buy all my shells in country stores and that these stores don't carry anything but 8s and 4s and the 8s are all dove loads.

If you can call them up into your lap and scrupulously eschew anything but head shots you can shoot them with 9s and kill them graveyard dead. Or 10s for that matter, if you can find 10s.

I do consider that any man has one overriding duty. I think that there is a firm obligation not to shoot at turkeys out of range.

A turkey is a hell of a big bird and an immensely strong one. The wing feathers, especially at the butt of the wing, are especially thick and strong and under them is a thick padding of breast feathers. Turkeys out of range ought to be let alone. Turning twenty-pound gobblers into wildcat food is a crime. No matter how badly a man wants a turkey, any turkey, he is in duty bound not to do this if he can help it. The best way of all not to do it is to let the long shots go.

There are not going to be all those opportunities for fancy wing shots on turkeys anyway. Doubles are fairly rare even where they are legal. The overwhelming number of turkeys are shot on the ground and the shotgun is handled about like a rifle. Most of the time you are sitting down; and all the niceties like forearm grip and cheek position and swing-past can be saved for the dove season next fall.

There are only two things you ought to be able to do. One is an absolute necessity and the other is a "consummation devoutly to be wished."

The first of these, the necessity, is the ability to be able to shoot from awkward positions.

Every discussion I have ever heard on shooting, or any training I ever had (and some of the training was of professional caliber) stressed at length the importance of getting comfortable. Just as in hitting curve balls, everybody says relax. They go on to talk about keeping the left foot slightly forward and mounting the gun smoothly and getting the stock to the shoulder in the same location every time. Whole chapters are written about the position of the cheek on the comb of the stock. Learned treatises both here and abroad point out that the cheek is actually the rear sight, and then go on at great length into fit and drop and stock length and so forth.

I am not laughing at a bit of this. On the contrary, I believe every word of it. And I have seen some good shots use it.

We have a man here in South Alabama named Billy Perdue. Billy has won the international live pigeon shoot in Spain several times. He is not just a good amateur shot, but a shot of international reputation. His work on doves will make you stand around with your mouth open, watching, and forget to shoot yourself. I know, and have shot with some more men here, who, while not in Billy's class, will make you weep with shame and frustration. All of these people do all the things you have to do to become good with a shotgun, including having shot the 10,000 rounds or so you have to shoot to become merely presentable.

None of them that I know of bother their heads for a minute about any of it on turkeys.

Turkeys, you see, are going to come up from behind you. They are going to walk up over your right shoulder. They are going to appear downhill, under your knees. You are repeatedly and regularly going to have to lean eight inches out of plumb either to the right or left to shoot around trees. You are

100

going to have to shoot with the stock mounted on your arm anywhere from the elbow to the collar bone. And you are going to be trapped into positions on downhill lies, that force you to keep yourself propped up with the left hand and shoot one-handed, the grip under the fore end being done with either knee.

Not a damned bit of this is going to require the same set of skills used to break 95 X 100 at trap. None of it at all is like the relaxed smoothness that regularly kills the limit of doves out of a box of shells. It does not have to be. What you are interested in here is not shotgun artistry, but the simple delivery of a charge of shot. A delivery effected often through a hole the size of a grapefruit, or through a slit like the crack between two loosely fitting barn doors. You normally only have to deliver it once, and except to ease the cramped position you may be delivering it from, you seldom have to do it in a hurry.

There are exceptions. Some second and third shots are going to have to be made quickly, though most third shots are only noise. Some of these second shots must not only be made quickly, but you are going to have to be getting up and scrambling sideways to make them. Remembering as you do it that this violates one of the foremost rules which says either shoot sitting down or standing up but never in between. Not only that, but when you sit down on the ground for an hour your knees get stiff, and your natural agility, whatever it may have been to begin with, is markedly reduced.

If you can deliver the first shot, regardless of the position from which you have to deliver it, it will be sufficient in 90 percent of the cases. This is the shot that shoes the baby.

The second half of this doctrine that I seem to be busily formulating after promising faithfully not to do so, the one that while not absolutely necessary is most highly desirable, is the ability to shoot from the left shoulder.

The first man I ever heard make this statement was and is a very close friend of mine. A man with whom I have hunted a lot, and a man who, if I had to get one turkey killed for a million dollars, I would go and try to get to kill for me.

The statement was made over bourbon, in front of a warm fireplace, and we were all very tired. Normally, remarks such as this put my back up. But in this situation and coming from such a source, and with the good whiskey and the warm fire (both his by the way) I let it pass. For one of the few times in my life I let what I considered to be a preposterous statement go unchallenged.

And Jesus, was I glad! The very next morning I had my nose rubbed in it.

Sit upon your rising sense of outrage and go along with me for a minute.

You are sitting down, with your back up against a tree. You have been in one position for over an hour; and there is a root you didn't find when you sat down that is precisely under the right cheek of your ass and is grinding up into the bone. Both legs are firmly asleep. As a matter of fact you are asleep from the waist down. Your gun, with your left hand under the fore end, is propped up on your left knee. Your right hand is on the small of the stock with your finger in the trigger guard. Both legs are bent so that your knees are propped up in front of you high enough to make the gun assume an angle of some forty-five degrees. You have achieved this position for several reasons. It lets you keep the gun partially presented all the time. It is as comfortable as any. If a turkey approaches from your left he is under the gun, and if he comes from directly in front of you, you can ease the gun from the left knee to the right, and at the proper time slouch down even lower and let the barrel down until it bears.

The direction in which you are facing is considered to be twelve o'clock.

A turkey gobbler, who has been keeping you pinned down for an hour and a half, steps around an oak tree, in plain sight at thirty yards.

At quarter after three.

If he were at quarter to nine, skill and intelligence would have again triumphed over ignorance and superstition. But he ain't. And your ass is named Dennis.

There is no earthly way you can get that gun around to him, right-handed. You can't swivel around; nobody but a contortionist could turn his waist far enough to do it. If you jump up, assuming the lack of circulation in your legs and feet doesn't put you face down in the leaves when you try, he will step back behind that tree before you get one tenth of the way up and you will have a splendid story to tell the boys in the barber shop. And if you think he is going to stand there and watch you squirming around sideways and crunching every leaf in sight until you can get the gun around to him, you ought to get your head looked into.

There are exactly two ways for you to kill him.

If you happen to be a practicing voodoo witch doctor, you can strike him dead with a glance. This, by the way, is a wonderful way to kill him. Not only does it save shells, which are so expensive nowadays, but it does not spoil the meat. Nobody is going to lay a lead shot on your wife's best china at the dinner when you eat him and look mournfully at you across the table while they feel for gaps in a two-hundred dollar inlay with their tongue.

If, however, you are a mere mortal, not skilled in witchcraft, or spells, or incantations, you can do one other thing.

You can very, very slowly, one inch at a time, carefully change hands and bring the gun up to the left shoulder, squinch up your right eye, look down the barrel, and bust his ass. Right where he stands. In the plain, old-fashioned, expensive way the rest of us do, with a shotgun.

That is, you could if you hadn't said "Horse shit" so firmly to the statement I made fifteen paragraphs ago.

I will accept at this time the retraction of that ugly word you used as gracefully as you would care to tender it.

It is not really hard to do. I taught myself to do it after the incident I just described happened to me. You don't have to be quick about it at all. Most of the time you can hear him coming a long time before you see him, and there is ample time to get the gun around even if you have to do it awkwardly and slowly.

And to be truthful, it is remarkably awkward at first. I have never tried to shoot from the left shoulder at anything flying. I have never even tried to shoot at anything moving from that position. But I can do it well enough on stationary targets to turn three o'clock turkeys into nine o'clock turkeys and that is sufficient. No man will kill a hell of a lot of turkeys who can't do it. It comes up more times than you would think it should, and not being able to do it is like playing golf without a sand wedge. You are going to hit one in the sand eventually that you can't pick off the top, and it is going to cost you the hole. Some rounds it will cost you two holes, because the gap you know is in your game will help you hit balls into sand traps.

Going through life being helpless in the face of three o'clock turkeys is not bright. By some subtle chemistry of the intellect they will find it out, and they will then parade up to you from that direction by battalions.

And now in summation of all these very firm pronouncements and iron bound rules and picky ass instructions, let me deliver the only final and absolute rule that must be followed to achieve membership in the Legion.

All in the hell you have to do is try.

There are dozens of men who will give you volumes of advice on turkeys, just as you can find dozens who will dissect your golf swing. You can get advice on yelping, advice on tactics, instruction on time and place. In spite of the fact that I began by swearing that I wouldn't, I have given some myself.

The world is full of books and of experts and of magic solutions.

I hunt with regularity and delight in the company of a good many men who are inept turkey hunters. They can't yelp. They get lost in the woods. The best day they ever had they couldn't tell north from straight up.

But they do the only really important thing and they do it exactly right. They go.

They go regularly and they go alone. They understand that it is a personal sport. They would be outraged if anyone offered to go with them and call a turkey up for them. They are not interested in execution or in ambush or in murder.

They hunt neither to accept gifts nor to be patronized. And to my mind they are far more admirable people than the men who fill their limit year after year, and then fill somebody else's.

In the beginning when you start, somebody has to teach you. Somebody has got to take the time and trouble to hunt with you, and to start you off, and to point you generally down the right road. Somebody has got to introduce you to turkeys in the beginning and take the trouble to present turkeys to you. This is at first. Afterward you are supposed to be on your own.

Whatever faults you have, or that you develop later on, you are supposed to puzzle out and correct.

To continue to be carried along, to continue to use another man to call, and to continue for years to let somebody else arrange turkeys for you, is the equivalent of that most doubly contemptible of enterprises, buying a piece of ass with somebody else's money.

The kind of men I am admiring generally kill one turkey on alternate Thursdays in alternate Aprils. And to be present at such an event is a delight. The rejoicing over the one sheep that returns to the ninety and nine is weak and thin by comparison.

Other hunters will gather round the turkey thus brought in and admire its fatness. They will carefully lift it up and judiciously heft it and will solemnly add three pounds to its weight. All moves to weigh the turkey, unless it is truly monstrous, will be firmly overruled. It is considered far better not to know.

Other hunters will greet each retelling of the story of the kill with the same rapt attention that was shown to Moses when he arrived with the tablets. And as with each repetition the story grows better, as the now picked and eaten turkey grows bigger, as the distance from which he was called lengthens, and as the pure tactical skill that was necessarily used to kill him approaches genius, they will deferentially agree.

Not only will they agree, but they will allude to difficulties they feel sure must have been overcome, but that the speaker in his innate modesty has forborne to mention. And they will bait out these difficulties, and exclaim over them in astonishment as each is surmounted in turn.

I will grow old, if I am lucky. My hair will grow white and my sinews wither. But long after I have crossed the threshold of senility, long after the sere and yellow leaves of my days have been piled and burned, this part of the sport will remain.

It may perhaps be the best part of it anyway.

I intend to lean upon my cane and stroke my white moustaches and enjoy it. With the fruits of a misspent life ripened and eaten and gone, and with no contemporaries around to correct my dogma, I shall most surely excel at these affairs.

I do pretty well at them now.

I am rather looking forward to it.

9

FINAL
THOUGHTS

Assume for a minute that you were the world's foremost authority on Amazonian orchids. Imagine, if you would, that for a period of several years the trade magazine, *Amazonian Orchidist*, had printed articles and features and entire serials about the possibility, only the possibility mind you, of the occurrence in the deepest recesses of the Matto Grosso of an extremely rare specimen. A specimen so rare that most other learned authorities went to some pains to deny its very existence. Imagine that you had carefully kept clear of one of those bitter internecine wars that commonly break out in botanical circles, but that the pros and cons had finally created such a schism within the association concerning the existence or non-existence of this new species, that ruin was imminent.

That finally, in order to settle the controversy and to bring peace to the pages of the trade journal, a delegation of your associates—you have no peers—had approached you, hats in hand, and begged you to take the time to go and settle the dispute.

Imagine then that you had agreed, and had spent time and money like water in flying to Brazil, interviewing natives, ferreting out rumors, and finally hiring trustworthy guides. Assume that you had finally after vast personal pain and anguish penetrated into the remotest parts of the upper reaches of the river, and had actually and in truth found there the most delicate and fragile black orchid possible to imagine.

A black orchid of such a splendor and of such breathless and ethereal beauty that the compulsion was almost overpowering to simply sit and worship it. That you had with the utmost skill and delicacy and care secured a single specimen, and that in a mad and breathless dash back down the river, through steaming and hideously dangerous jungles, had finally achieved the coast.

That there you had chartered, with no thought of expense, the fastest of all possible jet aircraft, and leaning heavily upon all your influence as an international scientific authority and world figure of letters, had prevailed upon the good offices of two great nations to permit you to take this national treasure out of Brazil and bring it home to the United States for the instruction and edification of the world's orchidologists.

Assume that you had landed it here safely in a transport of delirious delight. That you had accepted with suitable modesty the plaudits of the botanical world, had successfully quelled the mutiny, bound up the association's wounds and healed the schism.

And then, with the praises of every grateful orchidologist in the entire world ringing about your ears, at the very peak of your triumph, you had taken this rare jewel out into the backyard to show it to your goat—and he ate it.

Sic transit gloria mundi!

Meleagris gallopavo sylvestris is, among all the birds of the earth, such a jewel. One of our Creator's noblest efforts. Slim and bright—as light of foot and wing as fairy's breath. Quick and shy and wild, and a legend while he remains among us. And brought finally to bag and carried home in triumph, he is eaten.

Ground between the teeth, gnawed from the bone, made later into salads, and having the final fragments thrown out to the cat.

It is not right nor fitting nor proper that a bird who causes, simply by existing, a mystique, should suffer so plebeian a fate. But he does.

And the ultimate horror of it all is that when you do eat him he neither nauseates you nor sticks in your throat. He is perfectly delicious.

He is—and if that makes me an insensitive brother to the

goat, then I am sorry. Life honestly does go on and turkeys are roasted and eaten in it—really.

When Galahad found the Grail and bore it home in triumph to Camelot, the story ends. Stories end there as they should. They ought not to go on as life really does, in its usual homely and simple fashion after the triumph.

There is no record of how in later years Mrs. Galahad nagged him until he had to put down the paper and go and get the polish to shine it. Or how the little Galahads took it down from the mantel and dropped it on the brick hearth from time to time and dented its lip. Or of how they jarred some of its jewels loose from the settings and lost them under the sofa. Or of how he came home from a hard day killing dragons and found that they had taken it out into the yard and dug in the mud with it, and he had to scold them for it.

But they did.

For Grails and orchids and turkeys alike, pursued with the loftiest of motives, turn when captured into remarkably commonplace things. Food for either man or goat, or forms for children's mud pies.

Turkeys are really delicious, and I am wholly free of any of those foolish foibles which hold all wild game to be as nectar and ambrosia.

Ducks that have eaten mussels are atrocious. Venison that has been butchered hot, after having been run to exhaustion and eaten unaged, must be adulterated with cayenne pepper to kill the taste and make it barely edible. Woodcock, the best day they ever had, taste like worms.

Turkeys are invariably good. Simply picked and singed and stuck in the oven and roasted they are excellent. Twelve-pound yearling gobblers, stuffed with oyster dressing and served with wine, are nothing less than superb. The taste of all of them is so superior to that of a domestic turkey that such a turkey does not even belong in the same kitchen.

A wild turkey's legs are longer of course; he makes a living on them. The breast is not so broad nor is the white meat quite so white. But the moistness, and the texture, and the taste take you back to your boyhood. To the time when your taste buds had not been abraded by alcohol and tobacco smoke and years, and food tasted as it has not tasted since.

109

Compared to wild ones, domestic turkeys taste like oak sawdust mixed with clay.

Turkeys, though, are rarely shot to eat.

They are shot primarily for the pride of possession. There seems to be something about reducing one to the hand that appeals to some men to such a degree that in order to do so they will stoop to any meanness.

Turkeys are not shot from boats or from car windows simply to eat. They are shot to show and to talk about and to brag over.

Far too many men hunt turkeys seeking not the bird but the bubble reputation. And this is in truth a shame. For one of the strangest enjoyments in the sport comes from not killing turkeys.

I have killed some turkeys. God willing, I will kill a good many more of them. But there is a very strange and eerie phase of hunting turkeys. A phase that I have heard discussed very seldom. A phase that is alluded to frequently, but spoken of rarely—and that is the strange fact that it is possible to possess a turkey without killing him.

Upon rare occasions in the bull ring the matador is said to possess the bull. He does this when in the midst of the contest there springs into being a mystical union between man and beast—when neither seeks the death of the other any longer and they no longer fight, but minuet.

Upon even rarer cases in such situations, the crowd and the matador join, and in an outpouring of emotion, combine to give the bull his life for his bravery. And it is given to him freely, and not at the cost of the matador, nor to the matador's shame.

The situation I allude to with turkeys is not the same—quite. For it cannot be a gift—it must be taken. Turkey hunting differs principally in that, being such an intensely solitary sport, it lacks the crowd, and thereby eliminates much of the blood lust commonly engendered by mobs.

I have had it happen to me only very seldom, and then only with a big turkey, one I had gone to many times and with whom I had formed a kinship. In listening between the lines in discussions with a few other men, it seems that this is the only way it has happened to them either.

A man will find an old, big turkey. He will go back two or

three mornings and establish a contact every time. They, man and turkey, will duel with one another over a period of several days. Then somewhere around the fifth or the sixth day the game changes. There is no longer any obligation to kill the turkey. The desire to do so remains, but the obligation goes, and the entire affair moves into a different plane, almost a new dimension. No matter how the affair ends, the bird has now become the possession of the man.

In the beginning the man talks about it. He tells you one morning over breakfast that, "I have found one I can spend the season with." Two or three days later he will tell you, "He whipped my ass again," and he says it with admiration.

Then there will come the final stage when he will not discuss it. It has become too private to talk about, like a love letter. He is hunting now for the pure joy of the chase, for the intellectual exercise involved. The bird has not just become human—man and bird have become one—and they dance together.

This whole area is a most difficult subject to discuss. In the first place I do it with a peculiar feeling of nakedness. There are emotions best kept hidden. There is a degree of mysticism in it as well, and a degree of softness. And if you find it offensive, to hell with you—go and run your goddamn deer.

And it is always suspect—in the beginning.

When a man tells me of an affair like this, unless I know him very, very well, I instantly suspect intellectual dishonesty. The wholly ungenerous thought comes immediately into my mind that he cannot kill this turkey; so he says he doesn't want to. Only when I know the man can kill turkeys, and has done so regularly, and is a man of a certain temperament, will I accept it.

I read one time, I cannot now remember who wrote it or to whom the line should be accredited, that there should be a board appointed by the President—the President of the United States. That every person who proposed to paint or to sculpt should appear before this board, and be caused to do in its presence a horse and a hand.

A representational horse, and a hand that looked just like a hand.

That this person should be made to do this in order to have certified his draftsmanship and his anatomical discipline.

111

That only after his satisfactory appearance and performance, would a suitable certificate be issued by the board; and that only when in possession of this certificate would the individual be permitted to do abstracts—any abstracts.

The penalty for painted melted watches or straight lines, or for welding rusty bolts into grotesque lumps without being in possession of such a certificate would be punishable by death, or such other penalty as a courts-martial should adjudge.

I can't remember ever hearing such a splendid suggestion. It would differentiate between those who did because they chose, and those who did because they could do no other.

There are men to whom I would loan money, men that I would ask to hold my coat when I fought, men that I would trust with the keys to my wife's chastity belt while I went to the wars and men whom I would confidently leave in care of my baby girl.

But native suspicion will not let me accept the statement that a man has reached this highest plateau of turkey hunting upon his unsupported word. For this is a serious thing, and men who are often trustworthy in unimportant matters like sex and money and children are sometimes unreliable when it comes to turkeys.

This final peak is in such rarified air that many men never get there at all. I strongly suspect that there are men who have been there but who are afraid to admit it. They fear that it smacks somehow of over sensitivity. And has connotations of a mincing, simpering, emasculated and lace-pantied mentality.

I disagree with that. I consider it to be an honest emotion, honestly arrived at, only after a long apprenticeship.

I have been there. Not often but several times. And the first time I ever got there I let my ignorance spoil it.

There was a turkey gobbling in the northeast corner of a pasture. Two hundred yards east of the pasture fence, and running south in parallel with it, was a long gum pond. The first three times I went to him he would fly down, start south, and then get by me on one side or the other. I always went north to get to him, and if I sat near the pond he took the pasture route, and vice versa.

I formed the tactic of getting up after he had passed (he gobbled so much you always knew where he was) and getting out into the pasture beyond a little roll in the ground and running south to get around him. He always went south, and one morning I remember I got around him three times, and he got by me three times.

The ninth consecutive morning when he gobbled, I yelped, instantly got up and fell back, yelped and got up and fell back again. I never did wait for him—I took pains to yelp and leave before he could get near me. I moved in this fashion from a point near the northeast corner of the pasture, a full three quarters of a mile to the south end, always staying ahead of him as he came.

Level with the south end of the pasture, and two hundred yards since I had last yelped, I put my yelper down on the ground to remove the temptation to use it again, got into the middle of a tangle of ancient fence rails covered with vines, and waited.

In twenty minutes he was there, walking fast, in a half strut, and turning his head from side to side to look for me. He weighed twenty pounds if he weighed an ounce, and his wattles were as red as if his throat were cut.

I let him walk under the gun, with the safety off, at thirty yards and didn't shoot.

And ruined it.

For the past four days that turkey and I had possessed each other—and I had degraded him by letting him go.

I knew that I had ruined it the minute he was gone, for you may take all the pleasure you choose in losing, so long as you lose. You cannot throw the game.

He didn't even know I was there, but I did, and I cheapened him by giving him a gift he didn't ask for. I could not have demeaned him more if I had caught him by the foot in a steel trap and beaten his head off with an axe handle.

Killing turkeys is fun. But there is a far more satisfying feeling in driving home, drinking the last cup of coffee you have saved from daylight, and knowing he is still out there in the early sun, feathers gleaming as if he were freshly oiled, light and quick and wild, rather than a bundle of meat and feathers stiffening on the floor in the back seat.

But only if he has whipped you squarely. Only if you have

113

exerted every grain of skill, every trick of tactics, played every card you have, and lost.

I learned it then and I have never forgotten it.

I have it now, once and for all. Upon the few occasions I get up there again, if I ever do, I will know how to enjoy it and to revel in its rarity.

There is no reason why I will not be able to hunt turkeys for another forty years. It has become plain to me recently that sometime in my late seventies I may have to give up fall hunting. At the rate the hills are steepening lately they will be perpendicular by then, and the late seventies is no time to be taking up rock climbing. But I have met several old gentlemen in their eighties who were as deadly in the spring as ever, and I hope to become one of them.

The first turkey that ever came to me on the ground did it a long time ago. I sat there with my hands shaking and my breath short and my heart hammering so hard I could not understand why he could not hear it. The last turkey that came to me last spring had exactly the same effect, and the day that this does not happen to me is the day that I quit.

The last one that ever does come to me will call forth the same emotion that the second one did.

I will sit there waiting, gun up and heart thundering, and say to myself what I have said on every single occasion since the second one.

"I'm glad I lived to see it—one more time."

It is of course, a cult, and like all cultists we tend to be fanatics. Quick to take offense, defensive to the extreme, impatient of reason and logic, and with minds firmly closed and impervious to change. A cult that accepts novitiates carefully, rather than recruiting them. A cult whose members are mostly wet, often cold, and usually unsuccessful.

But the Legion's drum, like the Queen's, is always there, and its head is covered with shillings.

All you have to do to join is to pick one up.

We will be delighted to have you.